D0604569

DESIGN, BUILD,
EXPERIMENT

Chemistry Experiments

IN YOUR OWN

Laboratory

ROBERT GARDNER

Enslow Publishing
101 W. 23rd Street
Suite 240
New York, NY 10011
USA
enslow.com

Published in 2016 by Enslow Publishing, LLC
101 W. 23rd Street, Suite 240, New York, NY 10011

Cataloging-in-Publication Data

Gardner, Robert.
  Chemistry experiments in your own observatory / by Robert Gardner.
      p. cm. —(Design, build, experiment)
  Includes bibliographical references and index.
  ISBN 978-0-7660-6953-4 (library binding)
  1. Chemistry—Experiments—Juvenile literature. 2. Science projects—Juvenile literature.
I. Gardner, Robert, 1929–   . II. Title.
  QD38.G36 2016
  540.78—d23

Printed in the United States of America

To Our Readers: We have done our best to make sure all Web site addresses in this book were active and appropriate when we went to press. However, the author and the publisher have no control over and assume no liability for the material available on those Web sites or on any Web sites they may link to. Any comments or suggestions can be sent by e-mail to customerservice@enslow.com.

Portions of this book originally appeared in the book *Chemistry Projects With a Laboratory You Can Build.*

Illustration Credits: Jonathan Moreno; pialhovick/iStock/Thinkstock (graph paper background throughout book).

Photo Credits: Enslow Publishing, LLC

Cover Illustrations: Lisa F. Wang/Shutterstock.com (teen girl doing chemistry); wongwean/Shutterstock.com (science research background).

Contents

Introduction 5

Science Fairs 6

The Scientific Method 7

Chapter 1. Build a Chemistry Lab 9

Safety First 9

Build a Balance 16

Chapter 2. Chemistry and Weighing 21

☆ 2.1 Measuring Mass with Your Balance 24

☆ 2.2 Does Freezing Give Water More Mass? 27

☆ 2.3 Using Density to Identify Liquids 30

☆ 2.4 Identifying Solids Using Density 35

2.5 How to Weigh a Gas 39

☆ 2.6 Gas Density 42

Chapter 3. Chemical Reactions and
Their Speeds 48

3.1 A Chemical Reaction of Seltzer and Water . . . 49

3.2 Where Does the Gas in a Seltzer Tablet
Come From? 53

3.3 Making Chemical Predictions 55

☆ 3.4 Reaction Speed 56

☆ 3.5 Catalysts and Reaction Rates 61

3.6 Oxidation-Reduction Reactions 67

3.7 Electric Current and Ions 69

☆ 3.8 Oxidation of Iron: Rusting 73

3.9 Testing for Starch 75

3.10 A Forming a Precipitate 77

Experiments with a ☆ symbol feature Ideas for Your Science Fair.

Chapter 4. Acids and Bases **80**

    4.1 Litmus to Identify Acids and Bases 83

⭐ 4.2 Acid-Base Indicators 86

⭐ 4.3 Neutralizing with Acid 92

⭐ 4.4 Measuring Acidity 95

    4.5 Just for Fun: Chemical Magic 98

Chapter 5. Fun with Chemistry **100**

    5.1 Dancing Raisins 101

⭐ 5.2 Make a Genie in a Bottle 103

    5.3 Air Pressure and a Balloon 106

    5.4 Bubble Magic 108

    5.5 Vanishing Ink 110

⭐ 5.6 Secret Message 112

⭐ 5.7 A Jumping Flame 117

        Appendix: Science Supply Companies 121

        Further Reading 123

        Web Sites 124

        Index 125

EXPERIMENTS WITH A ⭐ SYMBOL FEATURE IDEAS FOR YOUR SCIENCE FAIR.

Introduction

Chemistry is the science of matter. Matter is anything that occupies space and has weight. Chemists investigate the make-up of matter, its properties, and how different kinds of matter combine. They know what makes things rust, how to remove stains from carpets and clothes, how insulation keeps food cold and homes warm, and much, much more.

Organic chemists study matter that contains carbon. Organic matter is found in plants and animals. Chemists can make many organic substances in the laboratory, too.

Inorganic chemists study all the other substances, such as water, air, metals, salts, acids, and bases. The experiments in this book focus mostly on inorganic chemistry. In order to do these experiments, you will first build a chemistry lab. Much of your laboratory work will take place in your kitchen. There you can find water, heaters, coolers, chemical tools, and many of the chemicals you will need.

At times, you may need a partner to help you. It is best if you work with friends or adults who enjoy experimenting as much as you do. In that way you will both enjoy what you are doing. **If any danger is involved in an experiment, you will be warned. In some cases, to avoid danger, you will be asked to work with an adult. Please do so.** Don't take any chances that could lead to an injury.

SCIENCE FAIRS

Some of the experiments in this book contain ideas you might use for a science fair. Those projects are indicated with a ☆ symbol. However, judges at science fairs do not reward projects or experiments that are simply copied from a book. For example, a diagram or model of an atom or molecule would not impress most judges; however, a unique method for finding out how the rate of a chemical reaction is affected by temperature or pressure would attract their attention.

Science fair judges tend to reward creative thought and imagination. It is difficult to be creative or imaginative unless you are really interested in your project; therefore, try to choose an investigation that appeals to you. Before you jump into a project, consider, too, your own talents and the cost of the materials you will need.

If you decide to use an experiment or idea found in this

book for a science fair, you should find ways to modify or extend it. This should not be difficult because you will discover that new ideas come to mind as you do experiments. You will think of experiments that could make excellent science fair projects, particularly because the ideas are your own and are interesting to you.

If you decide to enter a science fair and have never done so, you should read some of the books listed in the "Further Reading" section. These books deal specifically with science fairs and provide plenty of helpful hints and useful information that will help you avoid the pitfalls that sometimes plague first-time entrants. You will learn how to prepare appealing reports that include charts and graphs, set up and display your work, present your project, and talk with judges and visitors.

THE SCIENTIFIC METHOD

When you do a science project, especially one with your own original research, you will need to use what is commonly called the scientific method. In many textbooks you will find a section devoted to the subject. The scientific method consists of a series of steps.

1. Come up with a **QUESTION** or try to solve a **PROBLEM**. What are you curious about?

2. **RESEARCH** your topic. Find out what is already known. Has anyone already answered your question or solved your problem? What facts are published about your topic?

3. Form a **HYPOTHESIS**, which is an answer to your question or a solution to your problem.

4. Design an **EXPERIMENT** to test your hypothesis. Collect and record the data from your experiment.

5. Study your experimental **RESULTS** and form a **CONCLUSION**. Was your hypothesis true or false?

6. **REPORT** your findings.

All good scientific projects try to answer a question, such as "Does mass change when water freezes?" Once you have a question, you will need to form a hypothesis. Perhaps you think mass does change when water freezes. Your experiment should then test your hypothesis.

Scientific reports are very similar in format and include the problem, the hypothesis, the experimental procedure, the results, and a conclusion. You will follow a similar format when you prepare a report for your project.

Chapter 1

Build a Chemistry Lab

Chemistry, the investigation of matter, involves lots of experimenting. Experiments require equipment and materials. In this chapter, you will learn how to set up a safe area to be your chemistry lab.

Most chemistry labs have an area where chemicals and equipment are stored. Ask a parent or guardian if you can use or build shelves in your basement or garage to store chemicals and equipment. Also, ask if you can experiment in the kitchen. A kitchen makes a great laboratory. It gives you access to a sink, water, counter space, a heat source, a refrigerator, and a freezer. All these items are found in chemistry labs.

Safety First

Safety is essential in a chemistry lab. Your eyes require particular protection. They can be damaged by chemicals or flying fragments. Consequently, you should **always wear safety glasses** in the lab. Should any chemicals accidentally enter your eye, flood your eye with running water from the spray nozzle at your kitchen sink for at least ten minutes. Then tell an adult, and call a physician.

The likelihood of an injury is very small because most of the projects included in this book are perfectly safe. However, the following safety rules are worth reading before you start any project.

1. Do any experiments or projects, whether from this book or of your own design, under the supervision of a science teacher or other knowledgeable adult.

2. Read all instructions carefully before proceeding with a project. If you have questions, check with your supervisor before going further.

3. Maintain a serious attitude while conducting experiments. Fooling around can be dangerous to you and to others.

4. **Always wear safety goggles** in any chemistry lab, including your own.

5. Do not eat or drink while experimenting.

6. Have a first-aid kit nearby while you are experimenting.

7. **Do not mix chemicals just to see what happens!** You

might produce a poisonous gas, start a fire, or cause an explosion. Use only the chemicals called for and use or mix them only as directed.

8. Never let water droplets come in contact with a hot light bulb.

9. Never experiment with household electricity. Instead, use batteries.

10. Use only alcohol-based thermometers. Some older thermometers contain mercury, which is a dangerous substance.

11. Immediately use lots of water to wash off any chemicals that accidentally contact your skin.

12. Never insert glass tubing into the holes in rubber stoppers without wearing heavy gloves and first moistening the tubing and stopper with glycerin or liquid soap. Hold your hands close together to reduce leverage on the glass.

13. Similarly, in removing glass tubing from a stopper, carefully add a drop or two of glycerin to the hole before gently twisting the tubing. Wear heavy gloves. If the joint is really stuck, **ask an adult** to use a sharp knife to cut open the stopper.

14. Place heated glass on a piece of wood to cool. Never pick up hot glass. If in doubt, WAIT!

15. Do not use cracked or broken glass containers. To avoid injury to trash carriers, place broken glass in a can that can be sealed before discarding.

16. Always wear shoes, not sandals, in the lab.

17. Do not touch or taste chemicals unless instructed to do so.

18. Be careful not to mislabel chemicals or return a chemical to the wrong container.

19. **Wash your hands thoroughly** after finishing an experiment.

YOUR NOTEBOOK

Your notebook, as any scientist will tell you, is a valuable possession. It should contain ideas you may have as you experiment, sketches you draw, calculations you make, and hypotheses you may propose. A hypothesis is an idea you have about the reason something happens. Any hypothesis you have should be tested with an experiment to see if your hypothesis makes sense. Your notebook should include a description of every experiment you do, the data you record, such as temperatures, pressures, volumes, masses, and so on. It should also contain the results of your experiments, calculations, graphs you draw, and any conclusions you reach based on your results.

Your notebook is a well-kept journal describing and reporting on your actions in the laboratory. It should contain enough detail so that anyone could read it and understand what you did, why you did it, and what you found. It is a document you should be able to return to at a later date, read, and understand.

CHEMICALS

You will need a variety of chemicals to perform the experiments in this book and other experiments of your own that you do for a science fair or for your own interest. Some of the chemicals may be found in your kitchen or bathroom. Others might be borrowed from your science teacher or purchased at a pharmacy, supermarket, or one of the science supply companies listed in the appendix. The chemicals listed in Table 1 should be readily at hand. Other chemicals can be obtained as needed for a particular experiment.

MATERIALS AND EQUIPMENT

Many of the supplies and equipment you will need can be found in your home, borrowed from your school, or purchased from local stores. You might want to buy some items such as thermometers, flasks, tubing, and a few chemicals from one of the science supply companies listed in the appendix. The materials listed in Table 2 should be readily available. Other less frequently used items can be obtained as needed for a particular experiment. Occasionally, you will need a partner to help you do an experiment. And, remember, **all experimenting should be done under adult supervision.**

alcohol (rubbing)	cooking oil	iodine, tincture of
ammonia, clear, household	cornstarch	seltzer tablets
aspirin	distilled water, rainwater, or soft water	kosher salt
baking powder	Epsom salts (magnesium sulfate)	vinegar, clear
baking soda	flour	water

TABLE 1: Some Chemicals You Will Need Frequently

bags, plastic	graduated cylinder, 100 ml, or metric measuring cup
balance that you build (See Building a Balance on page 16.)	jars, small, such as baby food or jelly jars
	litmus paper, red and blue strips
battery, 6-volt dry cell or 4 D-cells	marking pen
beakers, small glasses, or cups	masses: standard set of gram masses or identical paper clips or metal washers
bottle, 500 ml–1 L (1 pint–1 quart)	
containers, plastic, that can be sealed	medicine cups, 30-ml (1-oz)
cooking pot, non-aluminum with cover	notebook
	paper clips
glass or jar, wide mouth, 200- or 250-ml	paper towels
dropper	pens or pencils
flask or bottle, narrow-neck, 200-ml	ruler
funnel	safety glasses
glass stirring rod, drinking straw, or coffee stirrer	test tubes
glass tube about 10 cm long	thermometer, alcohol, –10°C–110°C

TABLE 2: Materials and Equipment You Will Need Frequently

Build a Balance

You will need a balance to weigh things. If you don't have a balance, you can make one from a yardstick.

1. **Ask an adult** to drill three small holes through the yardstick as shown in Figure 1a. The hole at the 18-inch mark should be slightly above the center of the yardstick. The holes one inch in from each end of the yardstick should be about ¼ inch above the lower side of the yardstick as shown.

2. Push a snugly fitting finishing nail through the middle hole. The nail is like the center of a seesaw. It is the pivot around which the balance can turn. Place the ends of the nail on two tall sand-filled cans that sit on a bench or table.

YOU WILL NEED

- AN ADULT
- DRILL AND BIT
- YARDSTICK
- RULER
- FINISHING NAIL
- SAND
- 2 TALL CANS
- BENCH OR TABLE
- 2 PAPER CLIPS
- COMMON NAIL
- 2 ALUMINUM PIE PLATES
- STRING
- CLAY
- STANDARD GRAM MASSES OR IDENTICAL PAPER CLIPS OR SMALL WASHERS

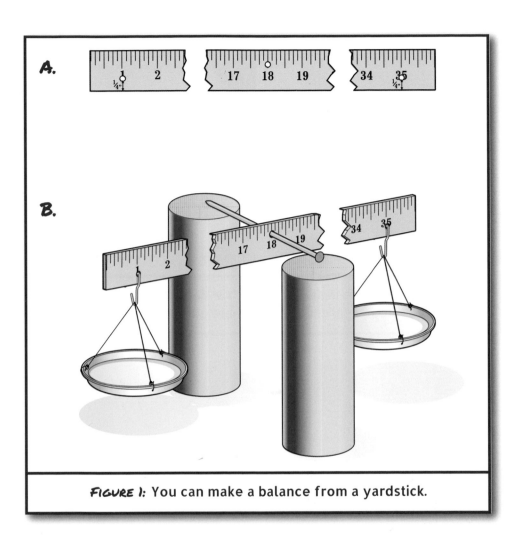

FIGURE 1: You can make a balance from a yardstick.

3. Open 2 paper clips. Slip the wider end of each clip through the holes at the ends of the yardstick beam.

4. Use a nail to make 3 equally spaced holes in the flat edges of each of 2 aluminum pie plates. The pie plates will serve as balance pans on which you can weigh things. You will need

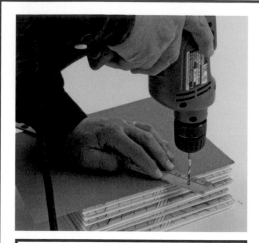

STEP 1. Ask an adult to drill three small holes in yardstick.

STEP 2. Push a nail through middle hole and place it on cans.

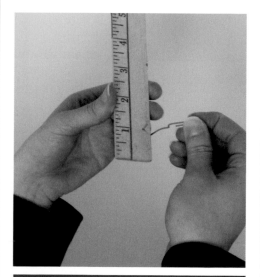

STEP 3. Slip paper clips through ends of yardstick.

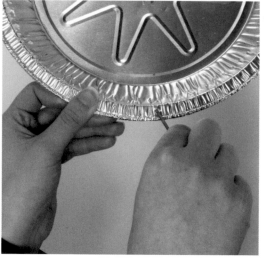

STEP 4. Punch three holes around edge of pie plate with a nail.

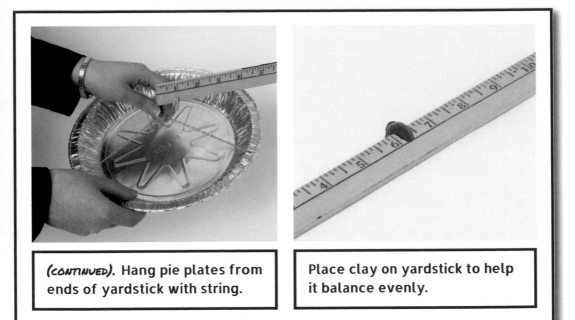

(CONTINUED). Hang pie plates from ends of yardstick with string.

Place clay on yardstick to help it balance evenly.

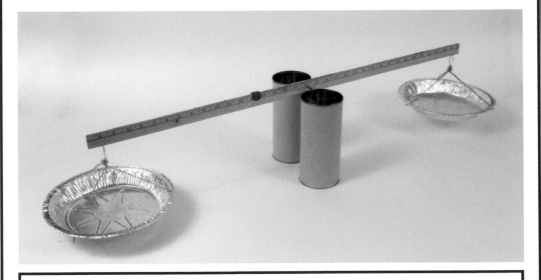

You have built a balance! Use the left-hand pan to weigh things and the right-hand pan for standard masses.

about a total of 4 feet of string to hang the pie plates. Cut the string into pieces as needed and attach plates to the paper clips at each end of the beam as shown in Figure 1b. If the balance beam (yardstick) is not level, add a small piece of clay to the lighter (turned-up) side. Move the clay closer to or farther from the center of the beam until the beam is level.

The balance will be used to weigh things placed on the left-hand pan. Standard masses will be placed on the right-hand pan until the beam balances (is level).

If you don't have a standard set of gram masses, you can use identical paper clips or small washers as your unit of mass. You will learn how to use paper clips or washers to measure mass in Experiment 2.1.

CHAPTER 2

Chemistry and Weighing

It is time to get started experimenting and using your homemade balance. If you do not have a set of standard gram masses, you will learn how paper clips or metal washers can be used to measure mass. After that, you will use your balance to start experimenting.

Before you begin experimenting, let's review the difference between mass and weight. It is something that many people find confusing.

MASS AND WEIGHT

To understand the difference between mass and weight, think about a pretend trip to the Moon. Suppose that on Earth your mass, as determined on a giant equal-arm balance, is 50 kilograms (kg). When you sit on one side of this giant balance, 50 kilograms must be placed on the other pan to make the balance beam level. So your mass is 50 kg. Your weight, however, is the force with which Earth pulls you toward its center (gravity). It is 490 newtons (N) (110 pounds). This weight can be determined by having you hang from a large spring scale or by standing on a bathroom scale.

When you reach the Moon, an equal-arm balance will show that your mass is still 50 kg. There is still the same amount of you. Your weight, however, as measured on a spring or bathroom scale, is only 81 N (18 pounds).

Why is your weight on the Moon only one-sixth as much as it is on Earth? The reason is that the force of gravity on the Moon is about one-sixth as large as it is on Earth. However, your mass, as measured on an equal-arm balance, remains the same. Both sides of the balance—you on one side, standard masses on the other—are both pulled toward the Moon with the same force. But the amount you stretch a spring is far less because the Moon's pull on you is only one-sixth as large as Earth's.

In other words, mass is the amount of matter in something. Weight is the force that gravity exerts on that matter.

To measure the mass of an object, place it on one pan of the balance (usually the one on your left). Known masses, based on the standard kilogram mass stored in Sèvres, France, are placed on the other pan until the balance beam is level. The level beam shows that the masses are equal. Because gravity pulls with the same force on equal masses, the effects of gravity cancel.

The kilogram is the standard unit of mass. The most common smaller unit is the gram (g), which is $\frac{1}{1000}$ of a kilogram. However, milligrams (mg), which are thousandths of a gram, are also commonly used. You may have seen pill bottles that give the mass of a chemical in milligrams. The U.S. customary system uses pounds, ounces, and a variety of other units.

Measuring Mass with Your Balance

If you do not have a set of standard gram masses, you can use identical paper clips or metal washers to measure mass.

1. You can figure out the mass, in grams, of a paper clip or washer quite easily. Just find out how many paper clips or washers equal one gram. To do this, place identical, empty, 30-mL medicine cups on opposite pans of the balance. If the beam is not level, move the clay until the beam is level.

2. Use a graduated cylinder or another calibrated medicine cup to add exactly 20 mL of water to the medicine cup on the left-hand pan. The mass of 1.0 L (1,000 mL) of water is very close to 1.0 kg or 1,000 g. (It varies slightly with temperature.) So, the mass of 20 mL of water is 20 g.

3. To find the mass of a paper clip or washer, add the paper clips

or washers to the right-hand pan of your balance until they balance the 20 g of water on the other pan. If you had to add 100 paper clips to balance the 20 g of water, then each paper clip weighs 0.2 g (20 g ÷ 100 = 0.2 g).

Suppose the last paper clip or washer you add tips the balance beyond its level position. How can you determine what fraction of that unit of mass is needed to exactly balance the beam? Can you figure out a way to measure fractions of a gram on your balance? (Hint: You can slide an open paper clip along the top of the yardstick.)

❤. Use your balance to measure a number of different objects. What is the smallest mass your balance can measure?

IDEA FOR YOUR SCIENCE FAIR

In building your balance, you were told to make the center hole at the 18-inch mark above the center of the balance beam. Why should that hole be above the center of the beam? What happens if the hole is below the center of the beam? How do the location of the fulcrum (middle nail) and the points from which the pans are suspended affect the sensitivity of any equal-arm balance?

THE LAW OF CONSERVATION OF MASS

There is a scientific law that states that matter is conserved. That means that matter cannot be created or destroyed. It means that there is no change in mass when substances change state (go from solid to liquid or liquid to gas). Nor does mass appear or disappear when substances combine chemically to form new substances. For example, hydrogen and oxygen gases react explosively to form water. According to this law, the mass of water will equal the combined mass of the hydrogen and oxygen that combined to form the water. Let's do an experiment that tests this idea.

Does Freezing Give Water More Mass?

Many eighteenth-century scientists believed that heat was a fluid, which they called caloric. One scientist, Benjamin Thompson (Count Rumford), believed that heat was simply the motion of molecules. He argued that if heat is a fluid, ice should weigh less than the water that froze to become ice. For water to freeze, it must lose heat. If heat is a fluid, as most eighteenth-century scientists believed, it seems logical to assume that water would lose mass when it freezes. You can test this idea for yourself.

YOU WILL NEED

- PLASTIC CONTAINER THAT CAN BE SEALED
- WATER
- PAPER TOWEL
- MARKING PEN
- BALANCE YOU BUILT
- A FREEZER

1. Find a plastic container that can be sealed. Partially fill the container with water and seal it. Wipe off any moisture from the outside of the container. Place the container on a level surface. Use a marking pen to mark the water level in the container.

2. Find the mass of the container as accurately as possible on your balance. Record the mass in your notebook. Put the container in a freezer. Leave it overnight so the water will freeze.

3. Remove the container from the freezer. Notice the level of the ice in the container. What happened to the volume of the water (the amount of space it takes up) when it froze?

Wipe off any moisture that condenses on the surface of the cold container. Then quickly find its mass. Has it lost mass?

Do you think the mass will change after the ice has melted?

4. After the ice melts, wipe off any moisture that condensed on the container and find the mass of the container again. What do you find? On the basis of your experiment, is heat a fluid that has mass? Was mass conserved when water froze? Was mass conserved when ice melted?

Idea for Your Science Fair

Do you think there will be any change in mass when sugar or salt dissolves in water? Design and conduct an experiment of your own to test your hypothesis. Was your hypothesis correct?

MASS AND DENSITY

Chemists often have to identify substances. The mass of a substance is not useful in identifying it. You can have a milligram or a ton of almost anything. However, knowing the mass of a certain volume can be very useful in identifying matter. We call the mass of a certain volume of a substance its density. Chemists usually measure the density of solids and liquids in grams per cubic centimeter (g/cm^3). Liquid densities are often expressed in grams per milliliter (g/mL); however, one milliliter has the same volume as one cubic centimeter, so they are really the same thing: 1 g/mL = 1 g/cm^3.

Using Density to Identify Liquids

The density of a liquid can be measured easily.

1. Measure and record the mass of a 100-mL graduated cylinder. Fill the cylinder to the 100-mL line with water. To measure the volume accurately, the bottom of the meniscus should just touch the 100-mL line as shown in Figure 2. If necessary, add or remove a small amount of water with a dropper.

2. Find the mass of the cylinder and the 100 mL of water. Based on what you learned in Experiment 2.1, what do you predict the mass of the water will be? Subtract the mass of the cylinder to find the mass of the water. Was your prediction correct?

Now that you know the mass and volume of the water, calculate the density of water in grams per cubic ml (g/ml), which is the same as g/cm^3.

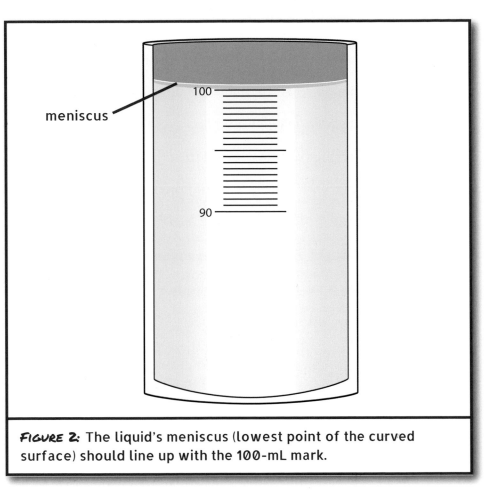

100

90

meniscus

FIGURE 2: The liquid's meniscus (lowest point of the curved surface) should line up with the **100-mL mark.**

$$\text{Density} = \frac{\text{mass, in g}}{\text{volume, in ml (or cm}^3)}$$

3. Find the density of rubbing alcohol. Is rubbing alcohol more or less dense than water?

4. Find the density of cooking oil. How does its density compare with the density of water? With the density of rubbing alcohol?

5. Pour a few milliliters of cooking oil into a glass of water. Are cooking oil and water miscible? That is, do they form a clear, uniform solution (a mixture that is the same throughout)? If they are not miscible, which liquid floats on the other?

Does the layering (one floating on the other) of water and cooking oil agree with what you would predict based on their densities?

6. Add a few milliliters of cooking oil to a plastic vial half filled with rubbing alcohol. Are these two liquids miscible? If they are not, which liquid sinks in the other?

Does the layering (one floating on the other) of alcohol and cooking oil agree with what you would predict based on their densities?

The densities of some clear liquids are shown in Table 3. If you used a balance that could measure to the nearest hundredth of a gram (0.01 g), would density be useful in identifying the chemical compounds known as acetone, methanol, ethanol, and isopropanol? How about if you used a balance that could measure to the nearest ten-thousandth of a gram (0.0001 g)? How confident would you be in using only density to identify one of these compounds?

Liquids	Density (g/mL or g/cm³)	
	Using a balance good to ± 0.0001 g	Using a balance good to ± 0.01 g
Acetone	0.7899	0.79
Ethanol	0.7893	0.79
Isopropanol	0.7860	0.79
Methanol	0.7914	0.79
Water	1.0000	1.00

TABLE 3: Densities of Some Clear Liquids at 4°C

IDEAS FOR YOUR SCIENCE FAIR

- Obtain four cans of cola in aluminum cans—regular cola, which contains caffeine and sugar; decaffeinated soda with sugar; decaffeinated diet soda (no sugar or caffeine); and diet soda with caffeine. Can you use density to distinguish among these four kinds of cola?

- You may have noticed that the bottle of rubbing alcohol was also labeled isopropyl alcohol. (It might also have been labeled isopropanol, another name for isopropyl alcohol.) But rubbing alcohol, by volume, is only 70 percent isopropanol. The other 30 percent is water. The density of isopropanol is 0.79 g/mL. Calculate the density of a mixture that has 30 mL of water and 70 mL of isopropanol. Compare your calculation with the density of rubbing alcohol that you measured. How might you explain any difference between your calculation and your measurement?

- What happens to the volume when ethyl alcohol and water are mixed? Can you offer an explanation?

Identifying Solids Using Density

Density can also be used to identify solids.

1. With a ruler you can measure the dimensions of a regular solid such as a wooden block. How can you find its volume from its length, width, and height? (Hint: The volume of a regular solid is equal to length × width × height.)

2. Find a block of wood. Measure and record its dimensions in your notebook. Calculate its volume. Then find its mass on your balance. Record its mass. Then calculate its density from its mass and volume (density = mass ÷ volume). How does its density compare with the density of water?

3. Do you think the wood will sink or float in water? Put it in a pan filled with water. Was your prediction correct?

YOU WILL NEED

- RULER
- WOOD BLOCK
- BALANCE YOU BUILT
- WATER
- STEEL OBJECTS SUCH AS WASHERS, NUTS, OR BOLTS
- 100-ML GRADUATED CYLINDER OR METRIC MEASURING CUP
- BRASS OBJECT
- 100 PENNIES
- CUBES OR CYLINDERS OF KNOWN METALS, SUCH AS ALUMINUM, COPPER, IRON, LEAD, AND ZINC THAT YOU MIGHT BORROW FROM YOUR SCIENCE TEACHER (OPTIONAL)

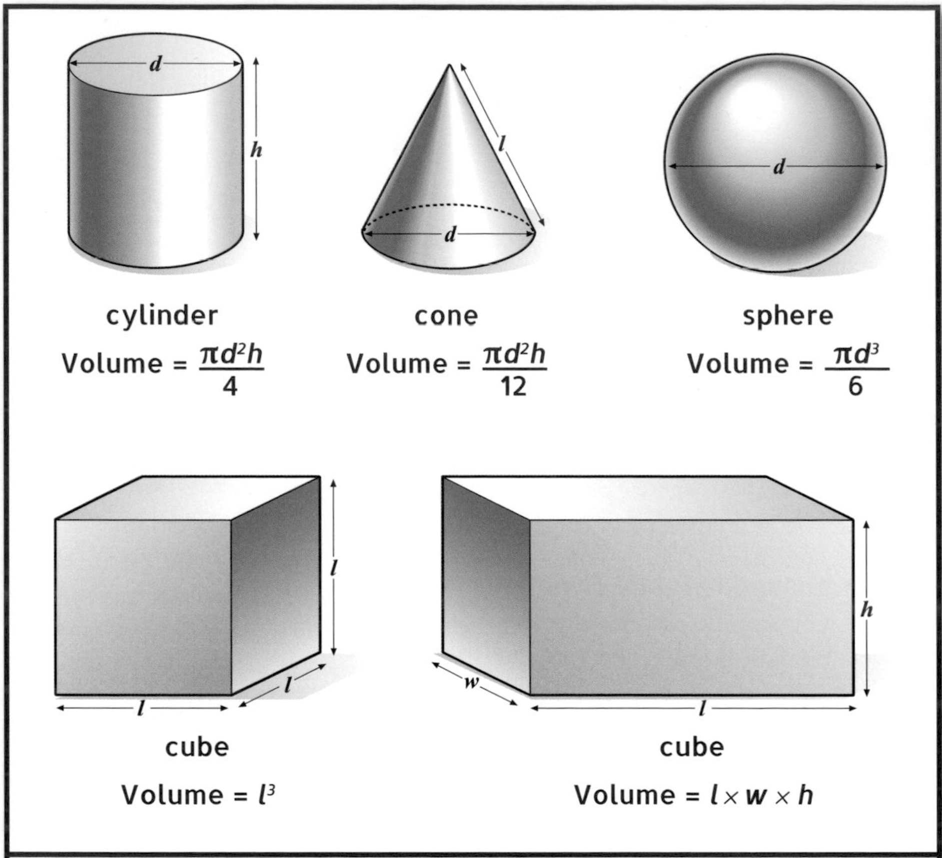

cylinder	cone	sphere
Volume = $\dfrac{\pi d^2 h}{4}$	Volume = $\dfrac{\pi d^2 h}{12}$	Volume = $\dfrac{\pi d^3}{6}$

cube	cube
Volume = l^3	Volume = $l \times w \times h$

FIGURE 3: You can find the volumes of some regular common shapes.

4. How would you use a ruler, a balance, and any other equipment you might like to use to find the density of a metal cylinder? A solid cone? A sphere, such as a baseball? You may find Figure 3 useful.

5. If possible, find some cubes or cylinders of known metals such as aluminum, copper, iron, lead, and zinc. Find the density of each metal. Then compare your findings with those in Table 4.

The volumes of irregular solids, such as stones, cannot be found using a ruler. However, as Archimedes discovered, their volumes can be found by measuring the volume of water each of them displaces.

6. You can use displacement to find the density of steel objects. Gather a number of identical steel washers, nuts, or bolts and find their masses. Then carefully drop them into a 100-mL graduated cylinder that contains 40 mL of water. If the water rises to the 90-mL line, you know the volume of the metal is 50 cm³ (90 cm³ – 40 cm³). Once you know the volume, how can you calculate the density?

Like many metal products, steel is an alloy, a combination of metals. Steel is primarily iron, but it contains small amounts of carbon and, often, other metals. How does your measurement of the density of steel compare with the density of iron shown in Table 4?

7. You may have heard that pennies are made of copper. Find the density of 100 pennies. Then compare that density with the density of copper found in Table 4. Do you think pennies are made of pure copper? Why or why not?

Solids	Density (g/cm³)	Solids	Density (g/cm³)
Aluminum	2.7	Lithium	0.53
Copper	8.9	Mercury	13.6
Gold	19.3	Nickel	8.9
Iron	7.9	Silver	10.5
Lead	11.3	Zinc	7.1

TABLE 4: Densities of Some Metals

IDEAS FOR YOUR SCIENCE FAIR

- Brass is an alloy (a mixture) of copper and zinc. Find the density of a brass object. Then determine the approximate percentage of zinc and copper in the brass object.
- Are hardwoods, such as oak and maple, more dense than softwoods such as pine?
- Obtain samples of different metals. Determine their densities and compare your results with Table 4.

How to Weigh a Gas

Weighing solids and liquids was easy, but can you weigh a gas?

YOU WILL NEED

- PLASTIC BAGS
- TWIST TIES
- YARDSTICK
- BALANCE YOU BUILT
- PLASTIC GARMENT BAGS
- WATER
- LARGE BALLOON
- SPRING BALANCE
- PLASTIC CONTAINER

1. Hang a plastic bag and a twist tie from both ends of your yardstick balance. Be sure the balance beam is level. Then fill one bag with air. Seal it with the twist tie, and reweigh it as shown in Figure 4a. Try not to make air currents as you make your weighings.

2. Perhaps you don't have enough gas to affect the balance. Try using large plastic garment bags. Fill one with air and again hang both bags from the ends of the balance.

You probably found that air appears to have no mass, but that doesn't seem right. You can feel it pushing you when the wind blows or when you run. It registers pressure on a barometer.

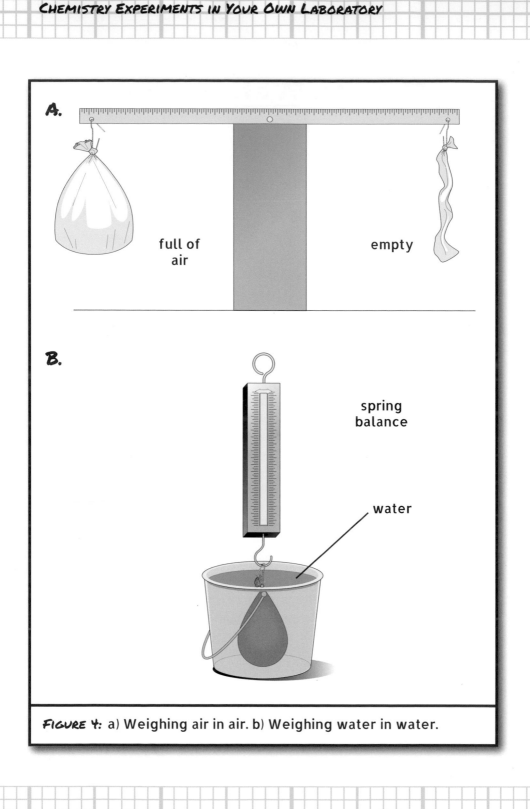

A.

full of
air

empty

B.

spring
balance

water

FIGURE 4: a) Weighing air in air. b) Weighing water in water.

3. To see why air appears to be weightless, try a similar experiment using water. Fill a large balloon with water. Seal its neck with a twist tie and hang it on a spring balance as shown in Figure 4b. How much docs it weigh?

4. Lower the balloon into some deep water in a plastic container. How much does it weigh in water?

Why does water appear to be weightless when weighed in water? The reason is that it is buoyed (lifted) upward by a force equal to the weight of the mass of water that it displaces. For the same reason, people can float in water. In air, a gas is buoyed up by a force equal to the weight of the mass of air it displaces. As a result, air appears to have no mass if weighed in air. Does this mean that it is impossible to find the mass of a gas? You can explore that question in the next experiment.

Gas Density

As you have seen, it is difficult to measure the mass of a gas. Gases have very small densities because a gas is mostly empty space. Its molecules are about ten times farther apart in all three directions than the molecules in a solid or liquid. As a result, its density is only about 1/1000 the density of a solid or a liquid. And, if you try to weigh a gas in air, the gas is buoyed up by the weight of the air it displaces. Since the density of air at room temperature is about 1.20 g/L, any liter

YOU WILL NEED

- AN ADULT
- SELTZER TABLET
- BALANCE YOU BUILT
- TWIST TIE
- TEST TUBE
- GRADUATED CYLINDER OR METRIC MEASURING CUP
- HEAVY DRINKING GLASS
- WATER
- PEN OR PENCIL
- NOTEBOOK
- RUBBER TUBING (ABOUT 50 CM LONG)
- ONE-HOLE RUBBER STOPPER TO FIT TEST TUBE
- HEAVY GLOVES
- GLASS TUBE ABOUT 10 CM LONG TO FIT INTO RUBBER STOPPER
- LIQUID SOAP
- LARGE BOTTLE, 500 ML–1 L (1 PINT–1 QUART)
- PLASTIC PAIL
- SQUARE PIECE OF CARDBOARD TO COVER MOUTH OF BOTTLE

of gas you weigh in air will appear to have a mass that is 1.20 grams less than its actual mass.

To weigh gases, chemists use a vacuum pump, a good balance, and a rigid vessel with a valve. They pump all the air out of the vessel, weigh it, and then let a gas flow into the empty vessel through a valve. After closing the valve and disconnecting the source of the gas, they reweigh the vessel. The increase in mass is the mass of the gas. Knowing the volume of the vessel and the mass of the gas they can calculate the gas's density.

But is there any way to measure the density of a gas if you don't have such sophisticated equipment? In some cases, the answer is yes. For example, seltzer tablets react with water to form a gas. If you weigh the water and seltzer tablet before and after the reaction, any loss of mass should be due to the gas that escapes. By collecting the gas, you can measure its volume. Knowing the mass and volume of the gas, you can calculate its density.

1. To carry out this experiment, break a dry seltzer tablet in half and place the pieces on the pan of your balance. Use a twist tie to hang a test tube with about 10 mL of water in it from the paper clip to which the pan is attached. (See Figure 5a.) The

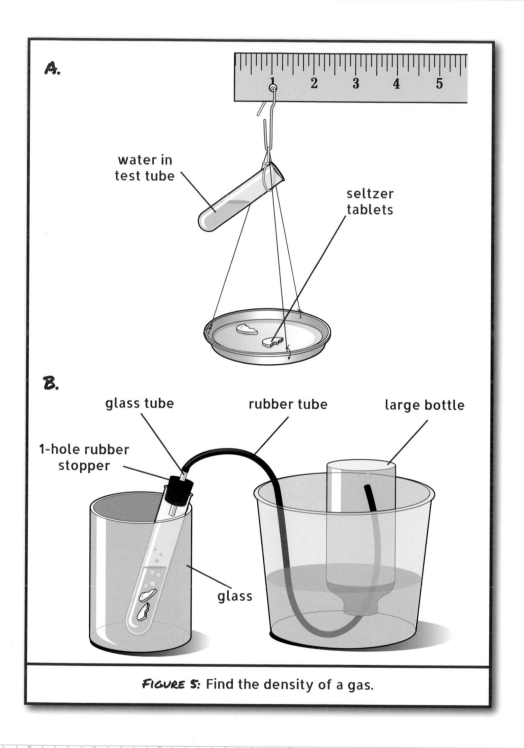

A.

water in test tube

seltzer tablets

B.

glass tube

rubber tube

large bottle

1-hole rubber stopper

glass

FIGURE 5: Find the density of a gas.

test tube should be about one-quarter to one-third full. Record the combined mass of tablet, test tube, and water.

2. Set up the apparatus shown in Figure 5b. (As you read on p. 11, **have an adult**, wearing heavy gloves, insert the glass tube into the rubber stopper. He or she may need to use liquid soap to help the glass tube safely slide into the stopper.) A heavy drinking glass can support the test tube. Fill the large bottle with water and fill the pail about one-third of the way with water. Cover the mouth of the bottle with a cardboard square. Hold the square against the bottle as you turn it upside down and put its mouth under the water in the pail.

3. Place the rubber tubing (about 50 cm long) inside and at the top of the inverted bottle of water.

4. Drop the pieces of tablet into the water in the test tube and immediately insert the one-hole rubber stopper into the mouth of the test tube. The glass and rubber tubes now connect two containers. The gas produced in the test tube as the tablet reacts will travel through the tubing to the bottle where it will collect as it displaces water from the large bottle.

5. Let the reaction proceed for about ten minutes. By that time the reaction will be nearly complete.

6. Remove the rubber tube that extends to the top of the bottle

before you remove the rubber stopper from the test tube. Otherwise, air may flow through the tubing into the bottle.

Cover the mouth of the bottle with the square piece of cardboard and remove it from the pail. Turn the bottle right-side-up and remove the square. How can you use a graduated cylinder or metric measuring cup to find the volume of gas that was produced? How can you find the mass of the gas? Record your data in a notebook.

7. Using the mass and volume of the gas, determine the density of the gas. What assumptions have you made in arriving at the gas's density? Could the gas be any of those shown in Table 5?

IDEAS FOR YOUR SCIENCE FAIR

- How might you find the density of other gases using

Gas	Density (g/L)
Air	1.20
Carbon dioxide (CO_2)	1.84
Helium (He)	0.154
Hydrogen (H_2)	0.083
Nitrogen (N_2)	1.16
Oxygen (O_2)	1.33

TABLE 5: Density of Six Common Gases at Room Temperature (20°C) and Air Pressure at Sea Level

a technique similar to the one you used in Experiment 2.6? After you have developed a plan, conduct your experiments under adult supervision.

- Table 5 gives the density of gases at a particular temperature and pressure. Do experiments to show how temperature and pressure can affect the volume of a gas. Calculate the change in density.

CHAPTER 3

Chemical Reactions and Their Speeds

When a chemical reaction occurs, there is a chemical change and new substances are formed. When these reactions take place, there is usually a release or an absorption of energy. Some chemical reactions, such as the rusting of iron, go very slowly. Others, such as the explosion of gunpowder, go very quickly. In this chapter, you will explore some of the factors that affect the speed of a reaction. Let's begin with the reaction of a chemical you can probably find in your home.

A Chemical Reaction of Seltzer and Water

1. Drop a seltzer tablet into a glass of water. What happens? What evidence do you have that a chemical reaction is taking place?

2. You can capture the gas that is produced when seltzer tablets react with water. Pour about 50 mL of water into a 200-mL narrow-neck flask or bottle. Break two seltzer tablets in half. Drop them into the water and quickly slip the mouth of a balloon over the top of the flask or bottle (see Figure 6a). What happens to the balloon as the seltzer reacts with water?

3. Use a small lump of clay to

YOU WILL NEED

- AN ADULT
- SELTZER TABLETS
- DRINKING GLASS
- WATER (COLD AND HOT)
- 200-ML (APPROXIMATE) NARROW-NECK FLASK OR BOTTLE (SCHOOL MAY HAVE FLASK)
- BALLOON
- CLAY
- BIRTHDAY CANDLE
- 200- OR 250-ML (APPROXIMATE) WIDE-MOUTH DRINKING GLASS OR JAR
- MATCHES
- A PARTNER
- LIMEWATER, A SOLUTION OF CALCIUM HYDROXIDE (OBTAIN FROM SCHOOL)
- A SAUCER
- ALCOHOL THERMOMETER, -10°C – 110°C

support a birthday candle in a wide-mouth 200- or 250-mL drinking glass or jar.

4. Have **an adult** light the candle. Let the candle burn until the flame is below the rim of the jar.

5. Squeeze the neck of the gas-filled balloon with your fingers so gas cannot escape. Twist the neck of the balloon around once or twice as you continue to squeeze. Remove the gas-filled balloon from the flask or bottle. Place the mouth of the balloon in the glass or jar next to the burning candle (see Figure 6b). Slowly release the gas from the balloon. What happens to the candle flame?

6. If any gas remains in the balloon, have a partner pour some limewater [a solution of calcium hydroxide $Ca(OH)_2$] into a saucer. Let the rest of the gas in the balloon bubble into the limewater. What happens to the liquid?

What gas do you think was in the balloon? Perhaps the contents of the seltzer tablets will help. All seltzer tablets, as their labels indicate, contain aspirin [$C_9H_8O_4$ (acetylsalicylic acid)], citric acid ($C_6H_8O_7$), and sodium bicarbonate [$NaHCO_3$ (baking soda)]. Sodium (Na) is a metal and could not form a gas with any of the other elements (hydrogen, oxygen, or carbon) at room temperature. So the most likely

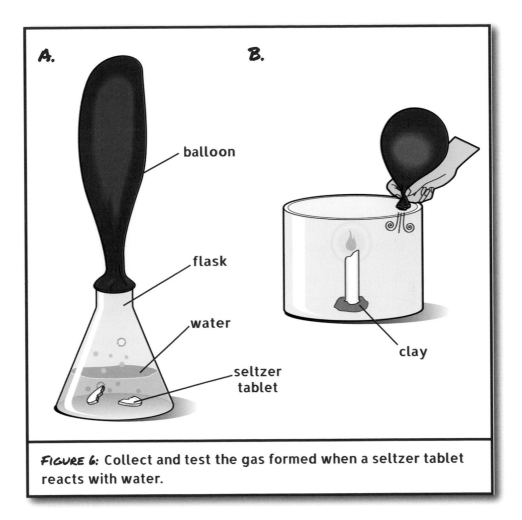

A.

B.

balloon

flask

water

seltzer
tablet

clay

FIGURE 6: Collect and test the gas formed when a seltzer tablet reacts with water.

gas possibilities are hydrogen (H_2), oxygen (O_2), carbon dioxide (CO_2), and carbon monoxide (CO). Hydrogen is a flammable gas that is much less dense than air. Oxygen is a gas that supports combustion (makes things burn fast) and is about the same density as air. Carbon dioxide is a gas more dense than air that is found in many fire extinguishers because

it does not burn and can smother flames. It will also turn
limewater milky because it reacts with calcium hydroxide
[Ca(OH)$_2$] to form calcium carbonate (CaCO$_3$), a white solid
that is not soluble in water. Carbon monoxide is a poisonous
gas, an unlikely product here since seltzer tablets are in
common use. Now, what gas do you think is produced when
seltzer tablets react with water? What makes you think so?

7. Is heat released or absorbed when a seltzer tablet reacts in
water? To find out, pour 50 mL of room-temperature water
into a 200-mL flask or bottle. Use an alcohol thermometer to
find the temperature of the water. Record the temperature.
Add two seltzer tablets. Watch the thermometer as the
reaction proceeds. Does the temperature increase, decrease, or
remain the same? What do you conclude?

Where Does the Gas in a Seltzer Tablet Come From?

Seltzer tablets contain aspirin [$C_9H_8O_4$ (acetylsalicylic acid)], citric acid ($C_6H_8O_7$), and sodium bicarbonate ($NaHCO_3$). (Some brands contain an additional chemical.) Which of the chemicals in a seltzer tablet react in water to form the gas? To find out, you can check them in a logical fashion.

You Will Need

- ASPIRIN TABLETS
- A SPOON
- CUP
- WATER
- CITRIC ACID (OBTAIN FROM SCHOOL OR SCIENCE SUPPLY HOUSE)
- SODIUM BICARBONATE (BAKING SODA)

1. Crush an aspirin tablet with a spoon. Then drop the powder into a cup of water. Does a gas form?

2. Repeat the procedure, but this time add sodium bicarbonate (baking soda) to water. Next add citric acid to water.

3. If none of the single ingredients reacts with water, try combinations of ingredients. Does a combination of aspirin and baking soda in water produce a gas? Does a combination of aspirin and citric acid in water produce a gas? How about baking soda and citric acid? Or do you need all three solids?

Based on your experiments, what do you conclude? Which chemicals in a seltzer tablet react in water to produce a gas?

Design and carry out an experiment to see if the gas is the same gas produced when a seltzer tablet reacts in water. What do you find?

Making Chemical Predictions

1. Examine the list of ingredients on a packet of Kool-Aid.

2. Predict what will happen when you add one teaspoon of Kool-Aid and one teaspoon of baking soda (sodium bicarbonate) to 100 mL of water in a glass.

3. Try it! What happens? Was your prediction correct?

4. Examine the contents on a package of Bromo-Seltzer. What do you predict will happen if you add some to a glass of water? Can you explain what happens? How does it compare with the addition of a seltzer table to water? Can you explain any differences?

YOU WILL NEED

- PACKET OF KOOL-AID
- TEASPOON BAKING SODA [SODIUM BICARBONATE (NAHCO₃)]
- GRADUATED CYLINDER
- WATER
- DRINKING GLASS
- BROMO-SELTZER

Speed of a Reaction

Can the speed (rate) of a reaction be changed? Are there things that can affect how rapidly a reaction proceeds? Let's look at some possible factors that might affect the speed of a reaction.

YOU WILL NEED

- GRADUATED CYLINDER OR METRIC MEASURING CUP
- COLD AND HOT TAP WATER
- 2 GLASSES
- SELTZER TABLETS
- PAPER AND PENCIL

TEMPERATURE

Atoms are very small particles. Molecules are made of atoms. Some molecules you may have heard of are oxygen (O_2) and water (H_2O). Both atoms and molecules move faster as temperature increases. For a chemical change to take place, atoms and molecules have to bump into one another (collide). How would an increase in temperature affect the number of molecular collisions per second? How do you think temperature might affect the rate of a reaction? Let's find out!

1. Pour 200 mL of cold tap water into a glass. Pour the same

volume of hot tap water into an identical glass. Drop a seltzer tablet into each glass at the same time. In which glass does the reaction go faster? Does temperature affect the speed of a reaction?

SURFACE AREA

How does the surface area of the reactants (the chemicals that react) affect the rate of a reaction?

1. Crush one seltzer tablet into small pieces on a piece of paper. Why does crushing increase the surface area? Leave a second tablet in one piece.

2. Put 200 mL of cold water into each of two identical glasses. Pour the crushed tablet into one glass of water. At the same time, drop the whole tablet into the other glass. In which glass does the reaction go faster? How does the surface area of the reactants affect the rate of a reaction?

AMOUNT OF REACTANTS

1. Pour 200 mL of cold water into each of two identical glasses. Into one glass drop a seltzer tablet. Into the second glass, drop half a seltzer tablet. In which glass is the amount of seltzer greater? In which glass does the reaction go faster? Remember,

if the reactions go at the same speed, it will take the whole tablet twice as long to react as the half tablet. How does the amount of reactants affect the speed of the reaction?

CONCENTRATION OF PRODUCTS

As you know from an earlier experiment, the reactants in this reaction are citric acid ($C_6H_8O_7$) and baking soda or sodium bicarbonate ($NaHCO_3$). The products, one of which you know, are carbon dioxide gas (CO_2) and sodium citrate ($Na_3C_6H_5O_7$). The chemical equation below summarizes the reaction. The reactants in a chemical reaction are always shown on the left side of the arrow. The products are shown on the right. The equation shows that for every 3 molecules of sodium bicarbonate that react with 1 molecule of citric acid, 1 molecule of sodium citrate, 3 molecules of carbon dioxide, and 3 molecules of water are produced.

$$3NaHCO_3 + C_6H_8O_7 \rightarrow Na_3C_6H_5O_7 + 3CO_2 + 3H_2O$$

3 sodium bicarbonate molecules	+	1 sodium citrate molecule	→	1 citric acid molecule	+	3 carbon dioxide molecules	+	3 water molecules

According to the law of conservation of mass, the number

of atoms of each element on the left side of the equation should equal the number on the right side. For example, there are 3 atoms of sodium (Na) on both sides of the equation and 9 atoms of carbon (C). Show that this is true for the other atoms (H and O) in the equation.

1. Now to the experiment. Pour 100 mL of cold water into each of two identical glasses. Drop two seltzer tablets into one of the glasses. Let that reaction proceed to completion. You now have one glass that contains products (carbon dioxide and sodium citrate) and one that does not.

2. Drop a single seltzer tablet into each glass. In which glass does the reaction go faster? How does the presence of products affect the rate of a reaction?

IDEAS FOR YOUR SCIENCE FAIR

- Do you think the amount of water will affect the rate at which a seltzer tablet reacts? Design and carry out an experiment to find out.

- Do you think seltzer tablets will react with liquids other than water, such as vinegar, alcohol, saltwater, and carbonated beverages such as cola? Carry out experiments to find out.

- Obtain some Bromo-Seltzer. It also reacts with water to form carbon dioxide. Weigh out an amount equal to the mass of one seltzer tablet. Predict which solid will react faster in water. Then check your prediction.

Catalysts and Reaction Rate

Some reactions go very slowly. Often the rate of such a reaction can be increased by using a catalyst. A catalyst changes the rate of a chemical reaction without being changed itself. Your saliva and the digestive enzymes in your stomach and intestines serve as catalysts in the digestion of your food. They accelerate the change of the large molecules in foods into smaller molecules that can pass through the intestinal walls and into the bloodstream.

YOU WILL NEED

- AN ADULT
- FORCEPS
- SUGAR (SUCROSE) CUBE
- A SINK
- MATCHES
- WOOD ASHES

In this experiment, you will use a catalyst to try to increase the rate at which ordinary sugar is oxidized (burned).

1. Use forceps to hold one end of a sugar cube over a sink. **Ask an adult** to bring a match flame near the other end of the cube in an effort to make the sugar burn. The sugar may melt, but it is not likely that it will burn.

2. Smear the end of the sugar cube with wood ashes from a

fireplace. Or **ask an adult** to obtain some ashes by burning some wooden matches or toothpicks. Now, **have the adult** try to ignite the ash-coated end of the sugar cube as you use forceps to hold the cube over a sink. What happens this time? How have the wood ashes affected the rate at which the sugar burns? Can you identify at least one of the products formed when sugar burns? If so, what is it?

IDEAS FOR YOUR SCIENCE FAIR

- Do some research. Find out what enzymes catalyze the digestion of carbohydrate foods. Where are these enzymes made? If possible, obtain these enzymes in powdered form. Use them to show that complex sugars are converted to glucose, a simple sugar, during digestion.
- Bile, which is secreted by the liver, is found in the small intestine. What role does bile play in the digestion of fats? Design an experiment to show how bile acts on fats.

SOME CHEMISTRY LEADING TO OXIDATION-REDUCTION

Chemists call the burning of sugar oxidation because substances burn by combining with oxygen. For chemists, oxidation is not limited to reactions involving oxygen.

Before you do experiments related to the broader meaning of oxidation, let's review some basic chemistry.

Matter is made up of atoms. There are about a hundred different elements, such as hydrogen, oxygen, iron, copper, helium, and so on. You will find all of them on a periodic table of elements that can be found in most chemistry labs and textbooks. Each element is made up of atoms that have a characteristic number of protons and electrons. For example, hydrogen atoms have 1 proton and 1 electron; oxygen atoms have 8 protons and 8 electrons; carbon atoms have 6 protons and 6 electrons. Each proton has a positive electric charge of $^+1$. Each electron has a negative electric charge of $^-1$.

Protons are found in an atom's nucleus, a tiny structure at the center of the atom. Most of an atom's space is empty but contains one or more electrons that move about the nucleus. Most nuclei (hydrogen atoms are the exception) also contain neutrons. Neutrons have about the same mass as protons, but they carry no electric charge. (See Figure 7.)

The mass of a proton or a neutron is nearly the same as the mass of a hydrogen atom. Chemists refer to it as 1 atomic mass unit (1 amu). The mass of an electron is only about 1/2000 the

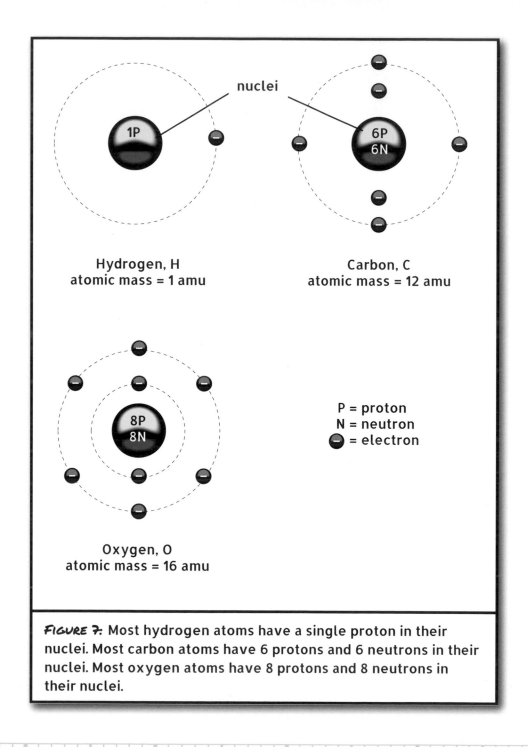

nuclei

1P

6P
6N

Hydrogen, H
atomic mass = 1 amu

Carbon, C
atomic mass = 12 amu

8P
8N

P = proton
N = neutron
= electron

Oxygen, O
atomic mass = 16 amu

FIGURE 7: Most hydrogen atoms have a single proton in their nuclei. Most carbon atoms have 6 protons and 6 neutrons in their nuclei. Most oxygen atoms have 8 protons and 8 neutrons in their nuclei.

mass of a proton. Electrons contribute very little to the mass of an atom.

Some electrons are farther from the nucleus than others. They are more easily lost than the electrons that are closer to the nucleus. For example, a sodium atom, which has 11 protons and 11 electrons, may lose an electron to a chlorine atom. When it does, it is left with 11 protons and only 10 electrons. As a result, it then has a charge of $+1$. The chlorine atom, by gaining an electron, now has 1 more electron than it has protons. It then carries a charge of -1. (See Figure 8.)

Atoms that acquire a charge are called ions. Sodium chloride is the compound that forms when sodium atoms give electrons to a chlorine atom. It consists of sodium ions (Na^{+1}) and chloride ions (Cl^{-1}) in a ratio of 1:1. Many other compounds are formed in this way. They are called ionic compounds because they are made up of ions. Other compounds form when atoms share electrons. Such compounds are said to be covalent.

Chemists define oxidation as the loss of electrons. Oxidation always goes with reduction, the gain of electrons. When sodium reacts with chlorine to form sodium chloride, the sodium is oxidized because it loses electrons to form

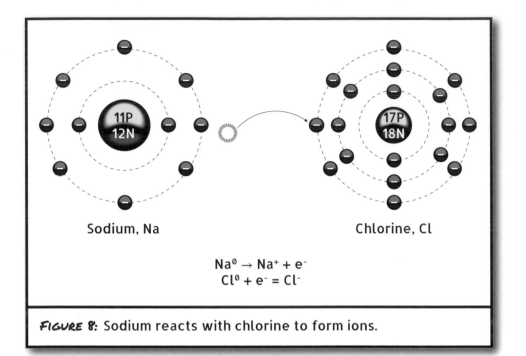

Sodium, Na   Chlorine, Cl

$$Na^0 \rightarrow Na^+ + e^-$$
$$Cl^0 + e^- = Cl^-$$

FIGURE 8: Sodium reacts with chlorine to form ions.

sodium ions (Na^{+1}). The chlorine is reduced because it gains electrons to form chloride ions (Cl^{-1}).

In the next experiment you will investigate an oxidation-reduction reaction in which an atom donates electrons to an ion.

Oxidation-Reduction Reactions

To begin, you need to prepare a saturated solution of copper sulfate.

YOU WILL NEED

- ABOUT 50 G OF COPPER SULFATE
- PAPER
- DISTILLED WATER, RAINWATER, OR SOFT WATER
- GLASS, PLASTIC CUP, OR BEAKER
- STIRRING ROD OR COFFEE STIRRER
- STEEL NAIL
- STEEL WOOL

1. Weigh out 50 grams of the blue crystals of copper sulfate ($CuSO_4 \cdot 5H_2O$) on a piece of paper.

2. Pour about 100 mL of distilled water, rainwater, or soft water into a glass, plastic cup, or beaker. Copper sulfate ($CuSO_4$) consists of copper ions (Cu^{++}), which have a charge of +2 (sometimes shown as $^{++}$) and sulfate ions ($SO^=$), which have a charge of –2 (sometimes shown as $^=$). Stir until most of the blue crystals dissolve. If necessary, add more crystals until no more will dissolve. Any excess copper sulfate can be left on the bottom of the container.

3. Find a steel nail (steel is mostly iron, Fe) that is taller than the container holding the copper sulfate solution. Rub the nail

with some steel wool to make it bright and shiny. Then put it into the copper sulfate as shown in Figure 9.

Y. After a few minutes, remove the nail. You can see that a reddish coat of copper has collected on the nail.

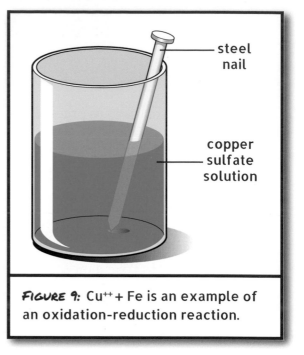

steel
nail

copper
sulfate
solution

FIGURE 9: Cu^{++} + Fe is an example of an oxidation-reduction reaction.

Since copper atoms (Cu) have no excess charge, the copper ions must have gained electrons to become copper atoms. The electrons must have come from the iron atoms, which were uncharged initially. The equation below summarizes what happened in this oxidation-reduction reaction. What was oxidized? What was reduced? (Sulfate ions are not shown because they are not involved in the reaction. Chemists call ions that are not involved in a reaction spectator ions.)

$$Cu^{++} + Fe \rightarrow Cu + Fe^{++}$$

Electric Current and Ions

As you know, ordinary table salt, sodium chloride, consists of equal numbers of positive sodium ions (Na^+) and negative chloride ions (Cl^-). Other compounds made up of positive and negative ions are also called salts, although they are not to be eaten. They include such compounds as potassium chloride, sodium iodide, copper sulfate, and so on.

You might think that salts, because they consist of charged particles (ions), will, like metal wires, conduct electricity. (Metals have electrons that can move easily from atom to atom.) To find out if they will, you can do the following procedure.

1. Nearly fill a clear plastic vial with table salt. Add two steel

paper clips, as shown in Figure 10a. Half of each paper clip should be inside the vial and half should be outside.

2. Connect the paper clips to a 6-volt, dry cell battery through a flashlight bulb in a socket. If you don't have such a battery, you can make one by placing four D-cells head to tail (Figure 10b) in a mailing tube. The tube should be slightly shorter than the total length of the four D-cells. Masking tape can be used to fasten steel paper clips or metal tabs firmly against the positive and negative terminals.

3. Connect the 6-volt battery to a flashlight bulb in a socket and to the paper clips on each side of the vial of salt as shown in Figure 10a. This can be done by using insulated wires that end in alligator clips. If you don't have a bulb holder, touch the metal base of the bulb with one wire and the metal side with a second wire as shown in Figure 10c. If you don't have wires with alligator clips, you can use clothespins to hold the ends of wires against the paper clips.

Does the bulb light? Does solid sodium chloride conduct electricity?

4. Perhaps a solution of the salt will conduct electricity. The water might allow the ions to move better. To find out, pour out half the salt and add water to nearly fill the vial. Reconnect

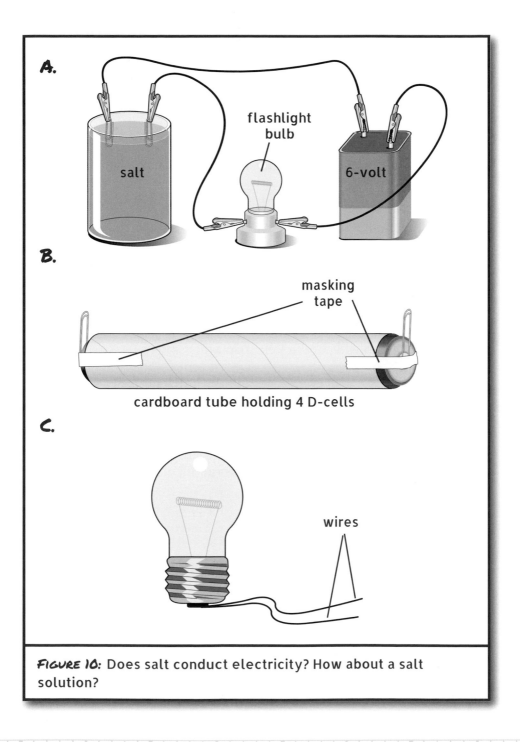

A.

flashlight bulb

salt

6-volt

B.

masking tape

cardboard tube holding 4 D-cells

C.

wires

FIGURE 10: Does salt conduct electricity? How about a salt solution?

the paper clips to the battery and a light bulb as shown in Figure 10a. Does the bulb light now? Can a solution of sodium chloride conduct electricity?

5. Will other salt solutions conduct electricity? To find out, you can try solutions of copper sulfate and Epsom salts [magnesium sulfate ($MgSO_4$)]. What do you conclude?

What about a covalent substance such as sugar ($C_{12}H_{22}O_{11}$)? (Its chemical name is sucrose.) It has no ions. The atoms in covalent compounds share electrons. Covalent compounds do not lose or gain electrons to become ions. Do you think a sugar solution will conduct electricity?

6. To find out, fill the vial you used before with a solution of sugar. Connect the paper clip electrodes to the battery and light bulb. Does the covalent sugar solution conduct electricity? Was your prediction correct?

Oxidation of Iron: Rusting

Another example of an oxidation-reduction reaction is the rusting of iron (Fe). Iron rusts when oxygen in the air slowly combines with it to form a compound called iron oxide (Fe_2O_3). The steel in steel wool is mostly iron, so you can use it in this experiment. Is the rate of the rusting reaction affected by the presence of different chemicals?

YOU WILL NEED

- SAFETY GLASSES
- STEEL WOOL (WITHOUT SOAP)
- SCISSORS
- WATER
- HOUSEHOLD AMMONIA
- VINEGAR
- CUPS OR GLASSES TO HOLD LIQUIDS
- PAPER TOWELS
- SOAP AND WATER

1. Cut a steel wool pad (one without soap) into 4 equal parts. Soak 3 of the pieces in different liquids for several minutes. Soak the first in water, another in household ammonia, and the third in vinegar. Let the fourth piece remain dry to serve as a control. **Warning: Do not put anything with ammonia in it near or in your mouth or eyes!**

2. After several minutes, remove the pieces from the liquids

and put them on labeled paper towels. Then wash your hands thoroughly.

3. Leave the samples for several days. Observe each piece from time to time to see what happens. Which one first shows evidence of rusting? Do any appear not to rust at all? Does an acid (vinegar) or a base (ammonia) seem to have any effect on the oxidation (rusting) of iron?

IDEA FOR YOUR SCIENCE FAIR

• When a candle burns, the wax in the candle is oxidized producing carbon dioxide (CO_2) and water (H_2O). Suppose a candle burns under a large beaker or jar so that there is a limited supply of air. Will the candle use up all the oxygen in the air before it goes out? Design an experiment to find out. Then, under adult supervision, carry out your experiment.

Testing for Starch

1. Add about ¼ teaspoon of cornstarch (or flour) to an empty glass, beaker, or plastic cup.

2. In another identical container about two-thirds full of water, add a few drops of tincture of iodine, **under adult supervision. Iodine is poisonous so keep it away from your eyes and mouth. Be sure to wash the containers and dropper thoroughly with soap and water when you finish.** Stir with a drinking straw to make a straw-colored liquid.

3. Pour the straw-colored liquid into the vessel that holds the cornstarch. Pour the liquid back and forth from one container to the other several times. What happens to the color of the liquid?

4. The color you see is a common test for starch. To see how

iodine can be used to test for starch in foods, try this. Mix about 10 drops of tincture of iodine with 100 drops of water. In separate dishes, crush or pour samples of potato, bread, milk, white meat (such as chicken breast), and a piece of an unsalted cracker.

5. Mix each of these food samples with a little water. Then test each sample with a drop of the iodine solution. **Remember not to put anything with iodine on it into your mouth!**

Which foods contain starch? How can you tell? What other foods might you try?

EXPERIMENT 3.10

Forming a Precipitate

YOU WILL NEED

- TEASPOON
- EPSOM SALTS
- WATER
- SMALL JARS
- GRADUATED CYLINDER
- STIRRING ROD OR DRINKING STRAW
- AMMONIA, CLEAR HOUSEHOLD
- COFFEE FILTER OR A PIECE OF FILTER PAPER
- FUNNEL
- TALL GLASS OR BEAKER
- PAPER TOWEL

1. Add a teaspoonful of Epsom salts to about 40 mL of water in a small jar. Stir until the salt dissolves.
2. Pour about 20 mL of household ammonia into the water. Do not stir! **Warning: Do not put anything with ammonia in it near or in your mouth or eyes!** Leave the chemicals to react slowly. In a few minutes, it will look as though a fog is forming within the liquid.
3. Look at the reaction periodically. What evidence do you have that a chemical reaction is taking place? Is the white substance you see more or less dense than the liquid around it?

The white substance is magnesium hydroxide. It is a precipitate (a solid that falls out of a solution). Can you separate the magnesium hydroxide from the liquid?

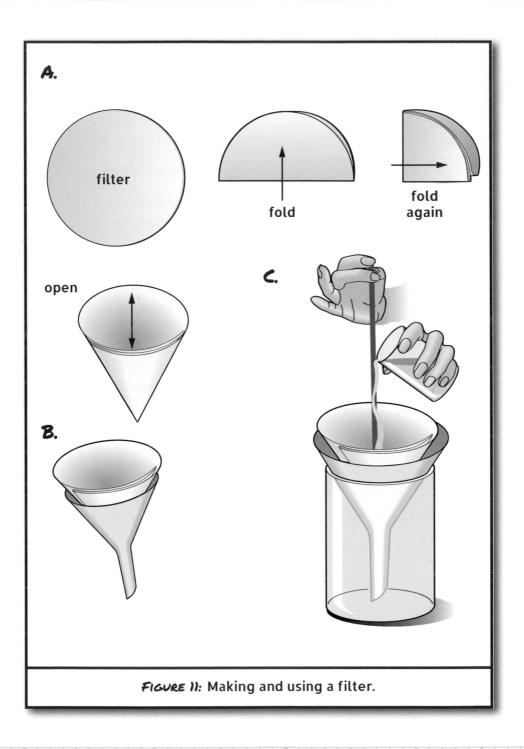

A.

filter

fold

fold again

open

C.

B.

FIGURE 11: Making and using a filter.

4. Fold a coffee filter or a piece of filter paper as shown in Figure 11a. Put the cone-shaped filter you have made inside a funnel (Figure 11b). Place the funnel on a tall glass or beaker.

5. Very gently pour the liquid and the finely divided white solid down a straw or glass rod onto the filter paper (Figure 11c). The filter has tiny pores in it. The pores allow particles smaller than the pores, such as molecules of water, to pass through. Does the filter prevent all the white particles from flowing through it?

6. Remove the filter paper from the funnel. Open it up and put it on a paper towel. Leave it there so the white solid on it can dry. Once it is dry, scrape it into a small jar. Cover the jar and save it for use in the next chapter.

CHAPTER 4

Acids
and Bases

You have now done some chemical reactions and have seen

that new substances are formed during these reactions. One

very common chemical reaction takes place between an acid

and a base. But what are acids and bases?

ACIDS

The Latin word for acid is *acidus*, which means sharp or sour.

Long before the birth of chemistry as a science, substances

that tasted sour were known as acids. Over time, substances

were called acids if they: (1) tasted sour; (2) dissolved in water

and formed solutions that conducted electricity; (3) contained

hydrogen that was released when the substance was added to

certain metals such as zinc; (4) turned blue litmus paper red;

(5) neutralized bases. *Neutralize* means the reaction of an acid

and a base to form a neutral substance (a salt) that is neither an acid nor a base.

From experience, you know that lemon juice and vinegar have a sour taste. Therefore, you might expect that these substances are acids and, indeed, they are. **Some acids are poisonous. Do not taste unknown things to see if they are acids.**

It is easy to see if a possible acid conducts electricity. Experiments like 3.7 will tell you. Such experiments show that sulfuric acid conducts electricity very well, whereas water is a very poor conductor. Vinegar (acetic acid) and lemon juice (which contains citric acid), are fair, but not good, conductors. For this and other reasons, sulfuric acid, found in car batteries, is called a *strong acid*, while vinegar and lemon juice are called *weak acids*. Water is not an acid. It is a neutral substance.

Acids react with zinc to form a gas. But, as you might guess, sulfuric acid reacts rapidly with zinc; vinegar and lemon juice react slowly. If the gas produced is used to blow bubbles in a soap solution, the bubbles ascend into the air like a bunch of small hot air balloons. This is because the gas produced is hydrogen, which is much less dense than air. You will explore the other properties of acids shortly, but first, what are bases?

BASES

Bases are also known as *alkalis*. The Medieval Latin word *alkali* means ashes. As you might guess, ashes have properties characteristic of bases. In general, bases have a bitter taste and feel slippery, like soap. Early American settlers made their own soap by boiling animal fat with lye [sodium hydroxide (NaOH)] that they obtained by leaching (washing) wood ashes. Bases, like acids, conduct electricity and neutralize acids. They turn red litmus paper blue. **Many bases are poisonous so you should not taste them.**

Litmus to Identify Acids and Bases

To test for acids and bases, you can use litmus paper strips. Acids turn blue litmus red; bases turn red litmus blue. Because it can be used to identify acids and bases, litmus paper is called an acid-base indicator.

1. Pour a few milliliters of vinegar into a small jar. Dip a piece of blue litmus paper into the vinegar as shown in Figure 12a. Does the litmus turn red?

2. What happens if you repeat the experiment with red litmus paper (Figure 12b)?

3. You could leach wood ashes to obtain a base, but it's much

YOU WILL NEED

- STRIPS OF RED AND BLUE LITMUS PAPER
- VINEGAR
- SMALL JARS SUCH AS BABY FOOD OR JELLY JARS
- CLEAR HOUSEHOLD AMMONIA
- LEMON JUICE
- APPLE JUICE
- GRAPEFRUIT JUICE
- CLEANSER POWDER (IN WATER)
- WATER
- RUBBING ALCOHOL
- SALT SOLUTION
- SUGAR SOLUTION
- ASPIRIN (IN WATER)
- WOOD ASHES (IN WATER)
- BAKING SODA (IN WATER)
- BAKING POWDER (IN WATER)
- LIMEWATER (CALCIUM HYDROXIDE)
- CITRIC ACID OR KOOL-AID CRYSTALS (IN WATER)
- WASHING SODA (IN WATER)

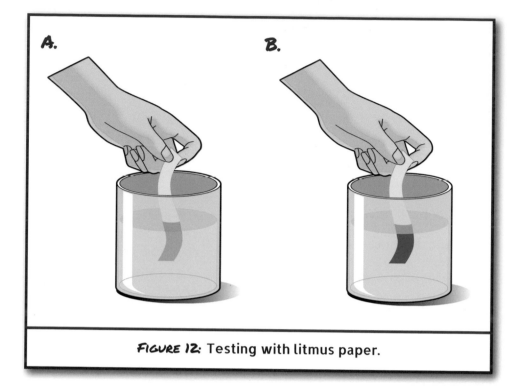

FIGURE 12: Testing with litmus paper.

easier to use a clear solution of household ammonia, which is also a base. Pour a few milliliters of the ammonia solution into a small jar. **Warning: Do not put anything with ammonia in it near or in your mouth or eyes!** Test as before with first red and then blue litmus paper. Which litmus paper changes color?

4. Use the litmus paper to test the other materials listed under "You will need." (Save these materials. You'll use them again in later investigations.) To test solids, add water to make a solution. Which of these substances are acids? Which are bases? Which have no effect on either red or blue litmus paper? Substances that are neither acid nor base are called neutral.

5. During Experiment 3.10, you were asked to save the white solid [magnesium hydroxide, [Mg(OH)$_2$] that you collected. Place the solid in a small jar or test tube and add a few milliliters of water. Is the magnesium hydroxide very soluble in water?

6. Test the mixture of magnesium hydroxide and water with litmus paper. Is it acidic, basic, or neutral? Label and save this mixture for testing with other indicators.

Acid-Base Indicators

Add lemon juice to a strong cup of tea. What happens to the tea's color? As you can see, tea is a natural acid-base indicator. There are many natural acid-base indicators. In this investigation you will explore some of them.

YOU WILL NEED

- AN ADULT
- RED CABBAGE
- CUP OF STRONG TEA
- NONALUMINUM COOKING POT AND COVER
- WATER
- STOVE
- FORCEPS
- REFRIGERATOR
- DROPPER
- SMALL JARS SUCH AS BABY FOOD OR JELLY JARS, VIALS, OR TEST TUBES
- WHITE VINEGAR
- CLEAR HOUSEHOLD AMMONIA
- LEMON JUICE
- APPLE JUICE
- GRAPEFRUIT JUICE
- RUBBING ALCOHOL
- SALT SOLUTION
- SUGAR SOLUTION
- CLEANSER POWDER (IN WATER)
- ASPIRIN (IN WATER)
- WOOD ASHES (IN WATER)
- BAKING SODA (IN WATER)
- BAKING POWDER (IN WATER)
- LIMEWATER (CALCIUM HYDROXIDE)
- CITRIC ACID OR KOOL-AID CRYSTALS (IN WATER)
- WASHING SODA (IN WATER)
- MAGNESIUM HYDROXIDE FROM EXPERIMENT 3.10
- UNSWEETENED GRAPE JUICE
- TUMERIC
- MEASURING SPOON
- GRADUATED CYLINDER

CABBAGE JUICE

The juice in red cabbage is a natural acid-base indicator. It can be prepared quite easily.

1. Take a few leaves from a red cabbage and break them into small pieces. Put them in a nonaluminum cooking pot. Add water to cover the leaves. Put a cover on the pot. **Ask an adult to help you heat the pot.** When the water is boiling, reduce the heat, but continue to boil the mixture for about half an hour. Then turn off the heat and let the water cool before removing the cabbage leaves with forceps.

2. Pour the cooled solution of cabbage juice into a container and cover it. Store the cabbage juice in a refrigerator.

3. Pour a few milliliters of white vinegar into a small glass jar. Use a dropper to add a few drops of cabbage juice to the vinegar. What is the color of the cabbage juice indicator in an acid?

4. Add a few drops of the cabbage juice to a few milliliters of ammonia. **Warning: Do not put anything with ammonia in it near or in your mouth or eyes!** What is the color of the cabbage juice indicator in a base?

5. Add a few drops of the indicator to some tap water, as shown in Figure 13. What is the color of the indicator? Is the water

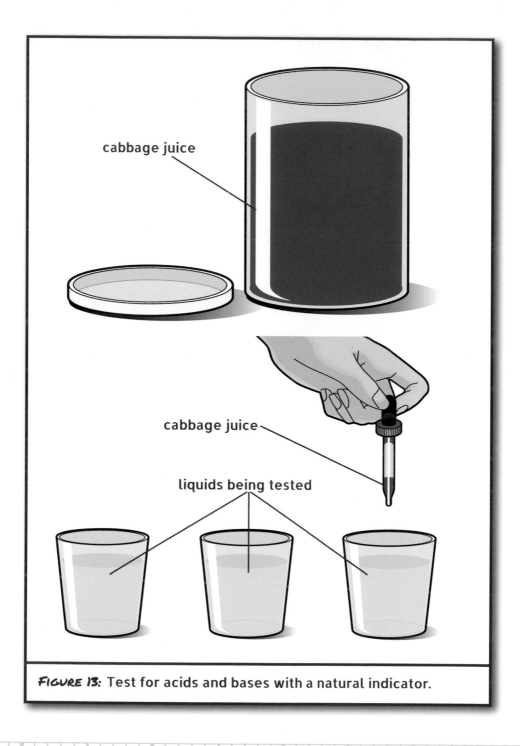

cabbage juice

cabbage juice

liquids being tested

FIGURE 13: Test for acids and bases with a natural indicator.

acidic, basic, or neutral? While pure water is neutral, water that comes from rain or the ground is often acidic or basic.

6. From the tests you did using litmus paper in Experiment 4.1, predict the color of the cabbage juice indicator in lemon juice, apple juice, grapefruit juice, alcohol, cleanser powder (in water), salt and sugar solutions, crushed aspirin dissolved in water, wood ashes mixed with water, solutions of baking soda and baking powder, limewater (calcium hydroxide), citric acid or Kool-Aid crystals dissolved in water, magnesium hydroxide, and washing soda crystals (in water).

Unsweetened Grape Juice

Unsweetened red grape juice is another natural acid-base indicator. It too should be stored in a refrigerator.

1. Add a few drops of unsweetened grape juice to several milliliters of white vinegar in a small jar. What is the color of grape juice indicator in an acid?

2. Add a few drops of grape juice to a few milliliters of ammonia. **Warning: Do not put anything with ammonia in it near or in your mouth or eyes!** What is the color of grape juice indicator in a base?

3. Add a few drops of grape juice to some tap water. What is the

color of the indicator? Is the water acidic, basic, or neutral? Why is cabbage juice a better indicator than grape juice?

4. From the tests you did using litmus paper and cabbage juice, predict the color of grape juice in lemon juice and all the other substances you tested before.

TURMERIC

Another natural indicator is turmeric, a common spice.

1. To prepare a natural acid-base indicator from turmeric, stir about ¼ teaspoonful of turmeric into 50 mL of rubbing alcohol.

2. Add a few drops of the turmeric solution to several milliliters of white vinegar in a small glass jar or test tube. What is the color of the turmeric indicator in an acid?

3. Add several drops of turmeric to a few milliliters of ammonia. **Warning: Do not put anything with ammonia in it near or in your mouth or eyes!** What is the color of this indicator in a base?

4. Add a few drops of the indicator to some tap water. What is the color of the indicator? Is the water acidic, basic, or neutral? Why is cabbage juice a better indicator than turmeric?

5. Based on your findings with other indicators, predict the color

of the turmeric indicator when added to the substances you have tested before.

IDEA FOR YOUR SCIENCE FAIR

Read the list of ingredients on a bottle of vitamin C tablets. Then crush one of the tablets into a powder and add some water. Divide the solution into four parts. Predict the color of litmus paper, cabbage juice, unsweetened grape juice, and turmeric solution when added to the vitamin C.

Neutralizing with Acid

One characteristic of an acid is its ability to neutralize a base. Similarly, one characteristic of a base is its ability to neutralize an acid.

YOU WILL NEED

- WHITE VINEGAR
- SMALL JARS SUCH AS BABY FOOD OR JELLY JARS
- CABBAGE JUICE INDICATOR
- PLASTIC SPOON OR STRAW
- DROPPER
- HOUSEHOLD AMMONIA
- BAKING SODA
- GRADUATED CYLINDER

1. Pour about 10 mL of vinegar into a small jar. Add a few drops of cabbage juice. Stir the mixture to obtain a uniform color throughout the liquid.

2. Use a dropper to add ammonia drop by drop to the vinegar. **Warning: Do not put anything with ammonia in it near or in your mouth or eyes!** Notice what happens to the color of the solution in the region where the ammonia drops land. Stir the liquid as you add the drops until you see a distinct color change. What has happened?

3. Now go the other way. Rinse your dropper and use it to add

drops of vinegar to the solution. Do this slowly. Notice the effect of one drop on the color of the solution. Can you see an intermediate color (purple) just before the solution changes from acid to base or base to acid? Remember, cabbage juice is purple in a neutral substance. If you can see the indicator turn purple, you are witnessing the exact point at which neutralization occurs.

4. What happens to the color of the neutral solution if you add a drop or two of vinegar? A drop or two of ammonia? **Warning: Do not put anything with ammonia in it near or in your mouth or eyes!**

Chemists define acids as proton donors. They define bases as proton acceptors. Remember, a hydrogen atom has a single proton and a single electron. An acid, such as hydrochloric acid, ionizes (forms ions) in water. Its ionization can be represented by the simple chemical equation shown below. As you can see, the acid provides a proton—a positive hydrogen ion (H^+)—and a chloride ion (Cl^-), so it has a proton it can donate.

$$HCl \rightarrow H^+ + Cl^-$$

A base, such as ammonia, forms hydroxide ions (OH^-) when it dissolves in water.

$$NH_3 + H_2O \rightarrow NH_4^+ + OH^-$$

During neutralization, the acid donates its proton (H^+) to the hydroxide ion. The hydroxide ion (OH^-) is a base; it accepts the proton to form water, a neutral compound.

$$H^+ + OH^- \rightarrow H_2O$$

This leaves water, ammonium ions (NH_4^+), and chloride ions (Cl^-). So if the water evaporates, it leaves a salt, ammonium chloride (NH_4Cl).

IDEA FOR YOUR SCIENCE FAIR

Cut three flat slices from an apple. Place them on a paper towel. Spread some citric acid or Kool-Aid crystals on one piece. Crush a vitamin C tablet (ascorbic acid). Spread it on the second piece. Leave the third piece exposed to the air as a control. Watch these pieces over a 24-hour period. What effect do these acids have on the chemical browning that occurs when apples are cut and exposed to air? See if you can predict what effect lemon juice would have on the browning reaction. Why do apples in a fruit salad that contains grapefruit, oranges, or other citrus fruits not turn brown?

Measuring Acidity

At the beginning of this chapter, you learned that sulfuric acid is a stronger acid than vinegar (acetic acid). It is a better conductor of electricity than vinegar. The degree of acidity of a substance is expressed as its pH. The pH of a substance is a measurement of the concentration of hydrogen ions provided by the acid. It is the concentration of hydrogen ions (H^+) that determines how well

YOU WILL NEED

- PH PAPER AND COLOR SCALE
- VINEGAR
- SMALL JARS
- WATER
- AMMONIA SOLUTION
- CLEANSER POWDER (IN WATER)
- BAKING SODA (IN WATER)
- LEMON JUICE
- GRAPE JUICE
- WASHING SODA (IN WATER)

an acid conducts electricity. The pH of a substance can be measured with pH paper, which contains several different acid-base indicators. The indicators in pH paper change color at different degrees of acidity, so the paper can measure a range of pH values. Neutral substances have a pH of 7. Substances with a pH less than 7 are acidic. A solution with a pH of 1 is very acidic; one with a pH of 5 is mildly acidic. Substances with a pH greater than 7 are basic. A solution with a pH of 14 is very basic; one with a pH of 9 is mildly basic.

1. Using pH paper, measure the pH of the substances listed in the materials list on the previous page. You may be able to borrow pH paper from your school or buy some at a hobby shop, a pool supply company (pH paper is used to measure the acidity of swimming pool water), or from a science supply company.

    Were you surprised to find that the pH of water was probably not 7? Most water, including rainwater, is slightly acidic.

2. What happens to the pH of vinegar if you dilute it by adding 10 mL of vinegar to 90 mL of water? What happens to the pH of the vinegar if you continue diluting it 1:10 with distilled water? What happens to the pH of ammonia if you dilute it in the same way with water? **Warning: Do not put anything with ammonia in it near or in your mouth or eyes!**

IDEAS FOR YOUR SCIENCE FAIR

- Use pH paper to measure the acidity of rainwater. Does the pH of rainwater in a long-lasting storm change with time?

Is the pH of the rainwater related to the size of the drops? Collect some snow and let it melt. What is the pH of snow? In a long-lasting snowstorm, does the pH of the snow change with time?

- Make two miniature "lakes" by pouring water into two wide soup bowls. What is the pH of the water in the two bowls? Pour some fine sand into one bowl; add an equal amount of limestone (calcium carbonate) to the other. What is the pH in each bowl after these solids have been added? Add 10 drops of vinegar to each "lake." What is the pH in each lake after the vinegar has been added? Continue adding vinegar and measuring the pH. What do you find to be different about these two lakes? Based on your investigation, would a lake with a sandy bottom or one with a limestone bottom be most affected by acid rain?

- Design an experiment to test the effect of pH on the germination of radish and bean seeds. Bear in mind that seeds will germinate on damp paper towels. Vinegar can be used to make tap water more acidic. Lime can be used to make tap water more alkaline.

Just for Fun: Chemical Magic

You can use acid-base chemistry to do some chemical magic for your family or friends. Tell them that you can change water to blood and then convert it back to water.

You Will Need

- **3 CLEAR VIALS, PLASTIC CUPS, OR SMALL GLASSES**
- **GLASS OR PLASTIC PLATE TO COVER ONE VIAL, CUP, OR GLASS**
- **WATER**
- **PHENOLPHTHALEIN (BORROW FROM A SCIENCE TEACHER)**
- **DROPPER**
- **WHITE VINEGAR**
- **AMMONIA**

1. To do this, first remove the cover from what appears to be an empty vial. After saying a few magic words, pour a clear liquid into it. The clear liquid suddenly takes on a deep reddish hue, which you call blood. Then pour the "blood" into another apparently empty vial and it will suddenly turn clear again.

The clear liquid is water to which you previously added 10 drops of phenolphthalein and 1 drop of white vinegar. The first "empty" vial actually contains 3 drops of ammonia. (The cover prevents the ammonia from evaporating.) **Warning: Do**

not put anything with ammonia in it near or in your mouth or eyes! The second "empty" vial contains 10 drops of vinegar.

Phenolphthalein is another acid-base indicator. It is clear in an acid and red in a base. The drop of vinegar in the water with the 10 drops of phenolphthalein makes the water slightly acidic. Consequently, the liquid is clear. When it is added to the vial containing 3 drops of ammonia, the ammonia, which is basic, causes the phenolphthalein to turn red, making it appear to be blood.

When the "blood" is poured into the second "empty" vial, which contains 10 drops of vinegar, there is enough acid to neutralize the ammonia and leave an excess of acid. The liquid becomes clear because phenolphthalein is clear in an acid.

In the next chapter you can have more fun using chemistry.

CHAPTER 5

Fun with Chemistry

Chemistry is not only a serious subject for school. It can be fun! You will agree when you learn how to make a flame "leap" through air, write invisible messages that appear when chemicals are applied, make ink disappear, produce magic bubbles, cause a "genie" to rise in a bottle, and make raisins "dance" in ginger ale.

You can have fun mystifying your family and friends with what to them will appear to be amazing. But what they see can be explained with your knowledge of chemistry. Whether you explain the chemistry or leave them mystified is up to you!

Dancing Raisins

Differences in density can explain what appears to be the "dance of the raisins."

YOU WILL NEED

- SMALL BUTTER KNIFE
- RAISINS
- DRINKING GLASS
- GINGER ALE, CLUB SODA, OR OTHER CLEAR CARBONATED BEVERAGE
- BUTTONS
- BAKING SODA
- VINEGAR

1. Use a small butter knife to cut 3 or 4 raisins into quarters.

2. Nearly fill a glass with a clear carbonated beverage from a newly opened can or bottle. The liquid should have plenty of carbon dioxide bubbles.

3. Add the raisins and watch them sink. Are they more or less dense than the liquid?

Soon they will rise to the top of the glass, float for a short time, and then sink back down. They will do this over and over. Can you explain why?

4. Watch one raisin closely as it moves up and down. Notice how the bubbles of gas cling to the raisin. As the bubbles accumulate, what happens to the density of the raisin and adhering gas? What happens when the bubble-covered raisin reaches the surface?

5. Do a similar demonstration using buttons in place of raisins and baking soda and vinegar in place of the carbonated beverage.

Make a Genie in a Bottle

This experiment involves density, as well as air pressure and convection (the movement of liquids and gases due to differences in temperature).

YOU WILL NEED

- GREEN FOOD COLORING
- INDEX CARD
- 2 NARROW-MOUTHED BOTTLES
- HOT AND COLD WATER

1. If you do this as part of a chemical show, add a few drops of green food coloring to one of the bottles *before* your audience arrives. Fill the other narrow-mouthed bottle to the very top with clear, cold, tap water.

2. Once your audience arrives, fill the bottle with the food coloring to the very top with hot tap water.

    You might tell the audience that a genie resides in the green-colored bottle and that you are going to try to coax her to emerge. Place an index card on the top of the bottle of clear, cold water before you turn it upside down and place it on top of the bottle with the hot, green liquid, as shown in Figure 14a. The water does not fall out of the inverted bottle because the index card, held in place by air pressure, keeps the water in the

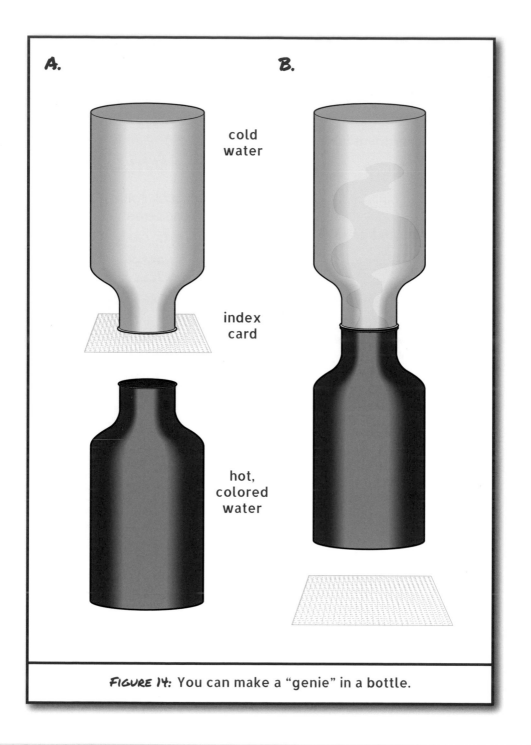

A.

cold
water

index
card

hot,
colored
water

B.

FIGURE 14: You can make a "genie" in a bottle.

bottle. (Air pressure can support a column of water 10 meters high as long as there is no air above the column.)

3. Carefully pull the index card from between the two bottles. Because hot water is less dense than cold water, a genie (the hot, green water) will emerge from the lower bottle and move into the upper bottle as shown in Figure 14b. Meanwhile, the cold water will sink into the lower bottle.

IDEAS FOR YOUR SCIENCE FAIR

- How is the density of water related to its temperature? Does its density increase all the way to its freezing point? What happens to the density of water after it has changed to a solid (ice)?

- What causes the water in lakes and ponds to "turn over" in many parts of the world during late autumn and early spring?

Air Pressure and a Balloon

This demonstration shows that air exerts a pressure that can push on things.

You Will Need

- AN ADULT
- CLEAR, EMPTY, RIGID PLASTIC BOTTLE WITH A NARROW NECK, SUCH AS A SOFT-SOAP REFILL BOTTLE
- BALLOON
- SMALL DRILL BIT AND DRILL OR A NAIL

1. Find a clear, empty, rigid plastic bottle with a narrow neck. **Ask an adult** to use a small drill bit or a nail to make a small hole in the bottom of the bottle. Next, put a balloon inside the bottle. Pull the lip of the balloon over the mouth of the bottle. (See Figure 15.)

2. Place your finger over the hole. Then ask someone to try to blow up the balloon. Of course, they can't. When they try, the air in the bottle is squeezed together and pushes back against the balloon. Say a few mumbo-jumbo magic words and then ask the person to try again. This time, without your finger over the hole in the bottle, he or she can easily blow up the balloon. Because the hole is open, the balloon, as it grows bigger, pushes the air in the bottle out through the hole.

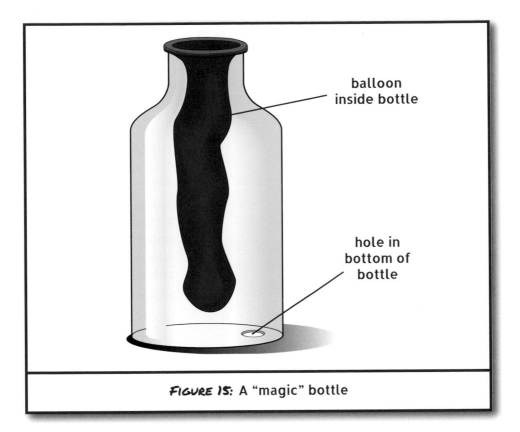

balloon
inside bottle

hole in
bottom of
bottle

FIGURE 15: A "magic" bottle

5. Put your finger over the hole in the bottle. When the person removes his or her mouth from the balloon, the balloon remains inflated. Actually, a small amount of air does leave the balloon so it gets a tiny bit smaller. In doing so, the air in the bottle takes up more space, so its pressure (push) becomes less than the pressure of the air in the balloon. As a result, the balloon remains inflated. What happens when you remove your finger from the hole in the bottom of the bottle?

EXPERIMENT 5.4

Bubble Magic

Before doing this demonstration, add about 50 mL of water, 10 drops of phenolphthalein, a squirt of dishwasher detergent, and 5 drops of household ammonia to a flask or bottle that holds about 250 mL (1 cup). **Warning: Do not put anything with ammonia in it near or in your mouth or eyes! The phenolphthalein in the presence of a base (ammonia) will cause the solution to be red. Put the flask on newspapers to protect any surface you are working on.**

Add two seltzer tablets to the flask. The sodium bicarbonate (NaHCO$_3$) and citric acid (C$_4$H$_8$O$_7$) in the seltzer will react to

YOU WILL NEED

- WATER
- PHENOLPHTHALEIN (BORROW THIS LIQUID INDICATOR FROM YOUR SCHOOL'S SCIENCE DEPARTMENT)
- DISHWASHER DETERGENT
- DROPPER
- HOUSEHOLD AMMONIA
- FLASK OR SMALL BOTTLE WITH A CAPACITY OF ABOUT 250 ML (1 CUP)
- NEWSPAPERS
- 2 SELTZER TABLETS
- GRADUATED CYLINDER

form carbon dioxide gas. The carbon dioxide forms carbonic acid (H_2CO_3) with water.

$$CO_2 + H_2O \rightarrow H_2CO_3$$

The citric acid and carbonic acid neutralize the ammonia and provide an excess of acid. Because phenolphthalein is clear in acid, the solution loses its redness. Bubbles form and emerge from the flask as the soap bubbles are filled with carbon dioxide gas. As the liquid loses its color, foamy bubbles will emerge from the flask.

Vanishing Ink

For this chemistry demonstration, you will need some household bleach [sodium hypochlorite (NaOCl)]. **Be sure to keep the liquid bleach away from your eyes, mouth, and skin!** Afterwards, be sure to thoroughly wash the container in which you placed the bleach.

YOU WILL NEED

- RUBBER OR PLASTIC GLOVES
- GLASS BEAKER OR PLASTIC CUP
- WATER
- DROPPER
- BLACK INK
- STIRRING ROD OR COFFEE STIRRER
- LIQUID HOUSEHOLD BLEACH
- CONTAINER TO HOLD BLEACH

1. Put on a pair of rubber or plastic gloves in case you spill some bleach. Hold a glass, beaker, or plastic cup so your audience can see that it is partially filled with water. Add a drop or two of black ink to the water and stir to make the liquid dark.

2. Pour a predetermined amount of a clear liquid (bleach) into the dark liquid and stir some more. After some stirring, the liquid turns clear.

3. Practice this demonstration a few times to find the exact volume of bleach you need to discolor the inky water. Bleach releases oxygen, which combines with the colored pigments in the ink to produce colorless compounds.

Secret Message

There are many ways to prepare invisible writing. Here are a few.

CHEMICAL MESSAGES

Because this kind of invisible writing requires a stove and the possibility of flames, it should be done under adult supervision. Keep a pan of water nearby. Should a piece of paper begin to burn, put it in the water.

1. Lemon juice is commonly used as an invisible ink. Use the wide end of a toothpick dipped in lemon juice to

YOU WILL NEED

- AN ADULT
- PIECES OF PAPER (10 CM X 10 CM)
- WATER
- HARD SURFACE SUCH AS A KITCHEN COUNTER
- STOVE OR HOT PLATE
- PAN
- LEMON JUICE
- TOOTHPICKS
- SUGAR
- TEASPOON
- MEDICINE CUP
- WARM WATER
- TONGS
- PAIL OF WATER
- COBALT CHLORIDE ($COCL_2 \cdot 6H_2O$) (OBTAIN FROM SCHOOL OR SCIENCE SUPPLY COMPANY)
- GRADUATED CYLINDER OR MEASURING CUP
- SMALL ARTIST'S BRUSH

write a message on a small piece of paper. Keep dipping the toothpick into the lemon juice as you write. There should be a continuous film of lemon juice along each letter you write. After you have finished writing the message, set the paper aside and let the "ink" dry.

2. While the lemon juice is drying, write another message on another small piece of paper. This time use saliva (something you always have with you) as the ink and another toothpick as your pen.

3. Write a third invisible message using a toothpick and a solution of sugar. To make it, add a teaspoonful of sugar to a medicine cup. Nearly fill the cup with warm water. Dissolve the sugar by stirring with the toothpick you will use to write the message.

4. When the "ink" on all your messages has dried, you will be ready to reveal the hidden messages. **Under adult supervision**, use a pair of tongs to hold each piece of paper, in turn, over a stove burner or hot plate as shown in Figure 16. Hold the paper well above the hot surface so that the paper doesn't burn. The message written in invisible ink will slowly appear on the paper. You can then show it to your audience.

All the "inks" used in these chemical messages contained

organic compounds (compounds that contain carbon). When heated, the organic substances partially decompose leaving substances that are visible.

FIGURE 16: Make invisible writing visible.

A BLUE MESSAGE

1. To write this invisible chemical message you will need to prepare a solution of cobalt chloride ($CoCl_2 \cdot 6H_2O$). Dissolve as much cobalt chloride as possible in 25 mL of water. The solution will be your ink. Write your message with a small artist's brush.

2. When the water in the solution has evaporated, tiny nearly invisible pink crystals of cobalt chloride will remain. **Under adult supervision**, use a pair of tongs to hold the paper over a stove burner or hot plate as shown in Figure 16. Hold the paper well above the hot surface so that the paper doesn't burn.

The message you wrote on the paper will appear in blue "ink." The pink crystals were hydrated; that is, they were chemically combined with water. Heating the hydrated pink crystals removed the water. What remained on the paper were the clearly visible blue crystals of anhydrous (without water) cobalt chloride ($CoCl_2$).

What happens to the message if it is left where moist air can reach it?

IDEAS FOR YOUR SCIENCE FAIR

- Sodium chloride (NaCl), ordinary table salt, is not an organic compound. It has no carbon. Heating dried salt will not produce a visible message, but can you find another way to use salt as an invisible ink?

- Develop invisible inks of your own. Use them to write secret messages.

A Jumping Flame

Because you will be using matches and working with a burning candle, this chemical demonstration must be done under adult supervision.

YOU WILL NEED

- AN ADULT
- CANDLE
- CANDLE HOLDER
- MATCHES
- LAMP CHIMNEY OR LARGE GLASS OR PLASTIC CYLINDER

1. Light a candle. Let it burn for several minutes. Then blow out the candle. Notice that a stream of light colored smoke continues to rise from the wick. The smoke is made up of hydrocarbon vapors from the wax. The vapors are flammable. Consequently, if you bring a lighted match to the stream of smoke several centimeters above the wick, the flame will follow the smoke stream downward and relight the wick.

For an audience, this demonstration is best done with a clear chimney lamp or a glass or plastic cylinder over the candle as shown in Figure 17. The top of the cylinder can be about 10 cm (4 in) above the wick. This will make the distance that the flame jumps more dramatic.

Figure 17: A leaping flame!

2. For an audience, you announce that you will blow out the candle and relight it without bringing a match to the wick. You then light a match, blow out the candle, and bring the match to the top of the chimney. There it will ignite the white vapor streaming from the wick. The flame will follow the smoke back to the wick. You can repeat this procedure several times, but let the candle burn long enough so that there will be good stream of vapor after the flame is blown out.

IDEAS FOR YOUR SCIENCE FAIR

- What is capillary action? How is it related to the burning of a candle?
- Let candles burn in inverted jars or beakers that vary in volume. How is the time that a candle will burn related to the size of jar or beaker?

Appendix: Science Supply Companies

Arbor Scientific
P.O. Box 2750
Ann Arbor, MI 48106-2750
(800) 367-6695
arborsci.com

Carolina Biological Supply Co.
P.O. Box 6010
Burlington, NC 27216-6010
(800) 334-5551
carolina.com

Connecticut Valley Biological Supply Co., Inc.
82 Valley Road, Box 326
Southampton, MA 01073
(800) 628-7748
ctvalleybio.com

Delta Education
P.O. Box 3000
80 Northwest Blvd.
Nashua, NH 03061-3000
(800) 258-1302
delta-education.com

Edmund Scientifics
532 Main Street
Tonawanda, NY 14150-6711
(800) 818-4955
scientificsonline.com

Educational Innovations, Inc.
5 Francis J. Clarke Circle
Bethel, CT 06801
(203) 748-3224
teachersource.com

Fisher Science
300 Industry Drive
Pittsburgh, PA 15275
(800) 766-7000
new.fishersci.com

Nasco
P.O. Box 901
901 Janesville Avenue
Fort Atkinson, WI 53538-0901
(800) 558-9595
enasco.com

Sargent-Welch/VWR Scientific
P.O. Box 92912
Rochester, NY 14692-9012
(800) 727-4368
SargentWelch.com

Ward's Science
P.O. Box 92912
5100 West Henrietta Road
Rochester, NY 14692-9012
(800) 962-2660
wardsci.com

Further Reading

Churchill, E. Richard, Louis V. Loeschnig, and Muriel Mandell. *365 Simple Science Experiments with Everyday Materials.* New York: Black Dog & Leventhal Publishers, 2013.

Dutton, Judy. *Science Fair Season: Twelve Kids, a Robot Named Scorch, and What It Takes to Win.* New York: Hyperion Books, 2011.

Eagen, Rachel. *Body Care Chemistry.* New York: Crabtree Publishing, 2011.

Editors of TIME for Kids Magazine. *TIME For Kids Big Book of Science Experiments: A Step-by-Step Guide.* New York: TIME for Kids, 2011.

Henneberg, Susan. *Creating Science Fair Projects with Cool New Digital Tools.* New York: Rosen Publishing, 2014.

Margles, Samantha. *Mythbusters Science Fair Book.* New York: Scholastic, 2011.

VanCleave, Janice. *Step-by-Step Science Experiments in Chemistry.* New York: Rosen Publishing, 2013.

Wheeler-Toppen Jodi. *Cool Chemistry Activities for Girls.* Mankato, Minn.: Capstone Press, 2012.

Web Sites

chem4kids.com
   Chemistry for Kids has basic chemistry help and
   information.

ipl.org/div/projectguide
   The IPL's Science Fair Project Resource Guide will help guide
   you through your science fair project.

**sciencebuddies.org/science-fair-projects/project_guide_
   index.shtml**
   Let Science Buddies give you extra ideas and tips for your
   science fair project.

Index

A

acetone, 33
acids and bases
    indicators, 86–91, 98–99
    litmus testing, 83–85
    neutralization, 92–94, 109
    pH measurement, 95–97
    principles, 80–82
air density, 46
air pressure, 103–107
aluminum, 38
ammonia, 84, 93–94, 98–99
Archimedes, 37
atomic mass unit (amu),
  63–65
atoms, 63–66

B

balance, building, 16–20
balloon, inflating, 106–107
bases. see acids and bases
bleach, 110
bubbles, 108–109
buoyancy, 39–41

C

cabbage juice, 87–89
calcium carbonate, 52
calcium hydroxide, 52
caloric, 27
carbon dioxide, 46, 51–52
carbon monoxide, 52
catalysts, 61–62
chemical equations, 58
chemical reactions
    catalysts, 61–62
    element identification,
      53–54
    predicting, 55
    product concentrations,
      58–59
    reactant amounts, 57–58
    speeds, 48–52
    speeds, factors affecting,
      56–60
    surface area effects, 57
    temperature effects, 52,
      56–57
chemistry, 5
chemistry labs
    building principles, 9
    chemicals, 13, 14
    materials, equipment,
      13–15
cobalt chloride, 115
cone volume, 36
copper objects, measuring,
  37, 38
copper sulfate, 67–68

cube volume, 36
cylinder volume, 36

D

density
    air pressure, 103–107
    displacement method, 37
    equation, 35
    gases, 42–47
    liquids, identification of,
      30–34
    mass and, 29
    metals, 37–38
    solids, identification of,
      35–38
    solubility, 32
disappearing ink, 110–111

E

electricity conduction, 69–72,
  81, 95–96
electrons, 63–65
enzymes, 61–62
ethanol, 33

F

filters, 78
flammability, 117–119

G

gas, weighing, 39–41
genie in a bottle, 103–105
gold, 38
gram masses, 20
grape juice, 89–90

H

helium density, 46
hydrogen, 46, 51
hypothesis, 12

I

ink, invisible, 110–116
inorganic chemistry, 5
iodine, 75
ionization, 92–94
ions, 65, 69–72
iron, 38, 73–74
isopropanol, 33

K

kilograms, 23

L

law of conservation of mass,
  26–28, 58–59
lead, 38
liquids, identification of,
  30–34

M

mass
  density and, 29
  law of conservation,
    26–28, 58–59
  measurement of, 24–25
  standard units, 23
  temperature and, 27–28
  weight vs., 21–23
metals, 37–38, 69
methanol, 33
milligrams, 23

N

neutrons, 63
nitrogen density, 46
notebooks, 12–13

O

organic chemistry, 5
oxidation-reduction reactions
  electricity conduction,
    69–72, 81, 95–96
  method, 67–68
  precipitate formation,
    77–79
  principles, 62–66
  rusting, 73–74
  starch, testing for, 75–76
oxygen, 46, 51

P

phenolphthalein, 98–99, 108
pH measurement, 95–97
precipitate formation, 77–79
proton donors, 93
protons, 63

R

raisins, dancing, 101–102
rusting, 73–74

S

safety, 9–12, 75, 81, 82, 84,
    108, 110
salts, 69
science fairs, 6–7
scientific method, 7–8
seltzer tablets, 43
shape volume equations, 36
solids, identification of, 35–38
solubility, 33
spectator ions, 68
sphere volume, 36
starch, testing for, 75–76
steel objects, measuring, 37
sugar (sucrose), 72

T

temperature

chemical reactions, 52,
   56–57
mass and, 27–28
Thompson, Benjamin, 27
turmeric, 90–91

V

volume, 36, 37

W

water, 32, 33
water to blood, 98–99

Z

zinc, 80–82